THE
7
HABITS OF

HIGHLY
DYSFUNCTIONAL
COMPANIES

JOEL DUBIN

About the Author

"This author definitely has seen many employees with work-related stress and mental health issues."
– Anonymous Psychiatrist

Joel Dubin is a retired cybersecurity consultant and recovering IT security auditor. His work brought him into contact with too many dysfunctional companies around the world. Dubin admits that he, in fact, holds an MBA from a prestigious business school, Kellogg at Northwestern University, but rarely mentions it in polite company. He is a widely known business crackpot and is fluent in several foreign languages, including gibberish. He lives in Chicago with his wife, Sara Guralnick, a children's book author and jewelry designer, with no kids or pets but an annoying bird clock that chirps every hour.

Acknowledgements

This book is dedicated to adult survivors of dysfunctional companies and the mental health professionals they keep in business.

They face a daily saga of aggravation, dashed dreams and spirits broken. Yet, despite being bandaged and bruised, they somehow survive yet another day.

"This guy, Dubin, is a business genius. I followed all the steps in his book and ran my business into the ground. Now I know exactly what not to do next time."
                    -- Someone leaving bankruptcy court

"Dysfunctional companies are like acid reflux. They keep coming up on you when you belch."
                    -- A businessperson

"Every now and then a business book about complete bullshit comes around. This is it."
                    -- Another businessperson

Early one morning, a man and a woman on their way to work step on an elevator. Their fists are clenched around the straps of their backpacks, and their jaws are tight. They're quiet and serious. They have an angry – ready for a fight – look in their eyes. They're already stressed, and they haven't even started work. A man leaning comfortably against the side of the elevator looks at them – relaxed and calm, probably retired or not working – and says, "So, which battlefield are you going to today? The academic or the company?" They mumble angrily under their breath, "the company."

This is their story . . .

Table of Contents

Introduction

The modern dysfunctional company is one of the greatest achievements of human history. Only the most brilliant minds in business could have conceived of such an ingenious way to manage an enterprise. In fact, the modern dysfunctional company isn't a brilliant new way to organize a business, at all. It's actually a carry-over from the Middle Ages.

The kings and queens, barons and nobles and knights of feudalism have been replaced by today's CEOs, managing directors, presidents and executives, vice presidents and directors, and managers. The modern-day equivalents of princes and princesses, aristocrats, clergy, and other sycophants, who sponged off royalty in the past are today's consultants, bankers, lawyers, and advisors and auditors, who leech off the dysfunctional company.

Just like their medieval counterparts, modern dysfunctional company warriors fight departmental turf battles, play politics and power games, and quarrel over staff headcount to feather bed their kingdoms and fiefs. No bureaucratic battle is too small. No pet project is too petty. No idea is too

1

stupid on the path to building an imponderable bureaucracy.

Their medieval counterparts wore armor, rode on horseback, and fought with swords. Today, they wear suits or dress in "business casual" and are armed with laptops and spreadsheets. Medieval knights have been reincarnated as so-called businesspeople whose modern playground isn't the feudal castle but it's equivalent – the dysfunctional company. They rule by hoarding power and building hierarchies. They use incomprehensible reports, bogus metrics and lawsuits to keep their power.

The business is secondary. The bureaucracy is primary. Jealously defending their sacred position within the bureaucracy is their goal. They aren't businesspeople. They're self-serving bureaucrats. They build moats around their company castles to keep out the barbarians – customers who are nothing but objects to be screwed.

The same feudal mentality that created the medieval world, created the dysfunctional company. The leadership philosophy of the dysfunctional company hasn't changed since the Middle Ages.

While the company lords and barons quibble and bicker, the serfs – today's employees – continue tilling in the company fields, hunched down in their cubicles and workspaces. The infighting of the aristocrats is behind closed doors, unseen by employees. The managerial chaos swirls around them, providing no leadership and no direction, sowing confusion, and chaos. Court jesters cleverly interspersed throughout the company, masquerading as HR and marketing, try to spread good cheer to no avail. Morale remains elusive at the dysfunctional company.

The Dysfunctional Company Can Be an Office or Remote

The dysfunctional company transcends space. It's not about where the company is located or whether the company has an office or works virtually. Its poison can be distributed either physically or virtually. It can be distributed between coworkers face-to-face or online in virtual meetings. It's about the relationships between its people, not the physical or virtual spaces they inhabit. The work environment is toxic, virtual or physical, affecting how it operates, and how it deals with the outside world.

It's not about its size either. The dysfunctional company comes in all sizes. It could be a small local company with only a few employees or a far-flung global empire with more employees than the population of a small country.

Ultimately, it's about how the company can't get anything done and produces no meaningful work. It peddles garbage products and services, and then uses its bureaucracy to fake looking good. The dysfunctional company is running on a treadmill – constantly in motion but going nowhere.

The Seven Habits of Highly Dysfunctional Companies

The modern feudal minds running the dysfunctional company have these seven simple bad habits to make sure the company doesn't move forward:

Habit One:
If It Makes Sense, Don't Do It

Habit Two:
Fighting Turf Battles Is Better Than Cooperating

Habit Three:
Poor Communication Delivers the Message

Habit Four:
If You're Not in A Meeting,
You Will Be Assigned to One

Habit Five:
Human Contact with Customers Is Prohibited

Habit Six:
Drive Out the Best Employees, Ignore the Rest

Habit Seven:
The Company Doesn't Serve the Common Good

Habit One:
If It Makes Sense, Don't Do It

The simplest most obvious way to do anything should be avoided at all costs. Any good ideas should disappear into sinkholes of committees, meetings, and reports. At some point, nothing gets done. **The Principle of the Appearance of Activity** is a fundamental rule explained in this chapter.

Habit Two:
Fighting Turf Battles Is Better Than Cooperating

The ideal company structure – pyramids with embedded silos – for increasing tension between business units and departments is covered in this chapter. Company organization to prevent cooperation and have departments working at cross purposes is key. The rules in this habit will not only stifle innovation but make sure communication will be constrained as explained in the next habit.

Habit Three:
Poor Communication Delivers the Message

The dysfunctional company can't overcommunicate. Everyone at the company should be bombarded to the point of annoyance with pointless e-mails and company announcements. The more irrelevant the better. How to use poor communication – particularly the excessive use of internal jargon and acronyms – is covered in this chapter.

The dysfunctional company uses language known only to its inmates – Company Speak. Even then, there is often a lot of confusion between different departments and business units, each often using their own dialects of Company Speak.

As an aside, it should be noted, in the spirit of the dysfunctional company, this book relies heavily on acronyms early on, in fact, starting with this chapter. The correct pronunciation of the acronym is also given, especially if not intuitive, often the case with dysfunctional communication. Some acronyms, of course, can't be pronounced and must be spelled out.

Habit Four:
If You're Not in A Meeting, You Will Be Assigned to One

It's far more important to plan until paralysis than to get anything done. Meetings are the main tool for achieving this goal. They're the lifeblood of the dysfunctional company. Between meetings and e-mails, the dysfunctional company strangles the life out of its employees. Add in forced socializing, irrelevant training and unnecessary team building activities and nothing gets done at work.

This habit will also cover the special case of remote employees and how their required attendance at meetings is enforced.

Habit Five:
Human Contact with Customers Is Prohibited

This chapter will cover the inner workings of Customer Disservice and how it makes sure customers, a sworn enemy of the dysfunctional company, are treated poorly, if treated, at all. Techniques for how to avoid customers and not provide adequate service are explained in detail. Punishments for employees who actually do talk to customers are also discussed.

Habit Six:
Drive Out the Best Employees, Ignore the Rest

The goal of the dysfunctional company is mediocrity. The best employees should be driven out. They should be replaced by clueless idiots who only follow instructions. HR policies and effectively hiring the worst employees is discussed in this chapter.

Office geography and organization guaranteed to antagonize employees and keep them in their place is also covered here.

This habit will also discuss the key role of remote employees, who form an important segment of the dysfunctional company workforce.

Habit Seven:
The Company Doesn't Serve the Common Good

Of course not. Why would the dysfunctional company serve anybody but itself? It's about greed, screwing employees and customers and not serving the common good. Mission statements? They're bullshit. It's about money, power and politics. Say one thing to the public and do something else. Hiding its bad behavior is the true strength of the dysfunctional company. It's about fooling the public and looking good.

A Word About Auditors . . .

Auditors and their role in creating an atmosphere of terror in the workplace are referenced frequently throughout this book in every habit. It's important to clarify the different types of auditors, their different roles in the dysfunctional company and how they're portrayed in this book.

Auditors come in many stripes. There may be financial and accounting auditors who examine the books to make sure there is no hanky-panky with company funds and assets. There may be IT auditors who regularly check to make sure IT systems are secure and running properly. There may be other ad hoc auditors, for example, peer reviewers, to make sure projects are on schedule and on budget.

Then, there may be an army of internal auditors who monitor compliance with external regulations. These same internal auditors may also police compliance with the extensive internal policies and procedures required by the dysfunctional company.

Everybody in the dysfunctional company, from executives on down to ordinary employees, has to deal with a maze of excessive and ridiculous internal policies and procedures just to get through the day. There are procedures for meetings, e-mails, required unnecessary training, project approvals, blowing your nose properly, filing expense reports and appropriate office behavior and having enough company swag on your desk or work area. This is just a sample of the auditable barriers to work mentioned in every habit. Be patient. There is more fun to come.

As will be seen throughout this book, it's the job of overzealous internal auditors to slap everybody, especially employees into line. Though this book refers to financial chicanery and broken or insecure IT systems, the auditors discussed here are mainly internal auditors harassing employees about inane company policies and procedures.

Two Levels of Dysfunctionality: People and Processes

In each of the seven habits, the dysfunctional company dysfunctions on two levels: processes and people.

On the process level, policies and procedures, such as bureaucratic obstacles, prevent employees from getting work done.

On the people level, the seven habits are about toxic work environments and the poor relations between people at the company. It's about the endless people problems endemic to the dysfunctional company. These are an essential part of every habit.

Sure, it might seem process problems are just people problems in disguise, since bureaucracies are staffed with people, who may have difficult personalities contributing to making the company dysfunctional. At times, the idiots in these positions may amplify the dysfunction.

Process problems may not necessarily be caused either by specific individuals, or surly personalities in key positions. The structure of the organization itself may block progress for even the sane and the competent who have miraculously managed to stay afloat at the dysfunctional company. Ideal company structures for keeping the company dysfunctional, and its culture toxic, are discussed in Habit Two about turf battles.

The dysfunctional company isn't just about executives and managers oppressing hapless employees, or creating a toxic work environment. It's more than that. It's a two-way street of bad behavior. Dysfunctional behavior permeates the organization at all levels. It's about how people interact not only between, but also within, different levels of the company. It's about how employees and management interact (in both directions – up and down the hierarchical ladder) with each other. It's about how executives and management treat their peers poorly.

Dysfunctionality affects the company both internally and externally. Beyond the internal chaos, it's also ultimately about how the company deals externally in poor relations with its customers.

The cardinal rule of the dysfunctional company: morons hire morons. The dysfunctional company tries to drive out its best employees, as discussed in Habit Six. It starts from the top down. Then it eventually works its way back up.

Dysfunctional management hires employees in their own dysfunctional image. By the time the company is fully staffed with idiots, it shouldn't be a mystery why the company is dysfunctional.

If it's not just how management treats staff, or how everybody treats each other, how can the dysfunctionality of a company be measured? No two dysfunctional companies are the same. However, they all have one thing in common that can be measured: the office asshole.

Before delving into the intricacies of measuring the asshole level of the company, called the **Asshole Density Ratio** or **ADR** for short, a firm understanding of the basic building block of the dysfunctional company, the **Pre-Assigned Work Station (PAWS)**, is required.

PAWS is the first acronym introduced in this book and should be written down in a safe location, or written a hundred times on a white board, until it's committed to memory. Likewise for the ADR, which should also be memorized. They will be used frequently throughout the book and should be scrawled on the bathroom walls at the dysfunctional company's offices. Their importance in dysfunctional culture can't be overstated.

The Pre-Assigned Work Station (PAWS)

PAWS range from long benches, at the lowest level, next to cubicles and finally up to private offices. The preferred PAWS in the dysfunctional company is a long bench with no dividers. Employees are packed shoulder-to-shoulder on top of each other in long rows, like cattle at a feeding trough.

Management euphemistically calls these "work spaces." They say it's for "collaboration." Instead, there are endless distractions from neighbors, not just immediate neighbors, but neighbors down the row. Loud phone calls, bodily noises, crunching on snacks and candy wrappers, downstream smells of body odor, all help employees get intimate and chummy, not necessarily collaborate.

There is no privacy.

Employees may find it difficult to call their psychiatrist – a common activity at the dysfunctional company – from their PAWS. They may have to go out to the parking lot just to make important calls.

This serves the main purpose of the dysfunctional company – keep employees distracted and off base, so they can't get any work done.

The next step up in employee placement through PAWS is the cubicle. Dysfunctional companies put employees in cubicle farms consisting of rows of cubicles out to the horizon. Floors upon floors with rooms packed wall-to-wall with cubicles are a part of the dysfunctional company landscape. The cubicle is the symbol of the dysfunctional company. It should be emblazoned on the company logo.

The cubicle in the dysfunctional company has its own culture and folklore, as will be discussed in Habit Six about employee abuse. Cubicles are more than just places to work. They're grouped in cell blocks, like in a prison, further subdivided into rows overseen by Row Captains, who oversee cubicle dwellers and enforce the many harsh policies so common at the dysfunctional company. The vital role of Row Captains is also covered in Habit Six.

Cubicles may have their own tribal feel, depending on their inhabitants. Different departments, especially those at war – common in the dysfunctional company, per Habit Two – may be decorated differently with their specific gang colors or insignia or banners with silly slogans. They may be adorned with warning signs telling outsiders, especially employees from other departments, not to intrude, or they may be turned over to audit or HR for punishment for trespassing.

The cold impersonal feel of cubicles is part of the dysfunctional environment. Cubicles may provide a little more privacy than open work spaces, but not much, since without doors, they're still exposed to noise and noxious odors from their neighbors. The height of the cubicle walls governs whether they stop nosy voyeurs and peeping Toms from peering over.

The only people with private offices are managers and above. Executives, particularly from the Cabal of Insiders, to be discussed in Habit Two about company stratification, may be in secured locations in ivory towers inaccessible to employees. Their offices may also be in underground bunkers to further insulate themselves from the rest of the company and the real world.

Whether private offices are only for mere mortal managers, or elite executives from the Cabal, the cardinal rule is: No farting. These offices are monitored with smoke detectors and evidence of flatulence will be logged and brought up during the manager's or executive's annual performance review.

For remote employees, their PAWS is where they set up their laptop. This could be any room in either their home, or a home office equipped just for work, to a shared office space or a coffee shop.

Wherever they are, however, even if in their own home, they're still not far from the clutches of the dysfunctional company. Monitoring software tracks their every movement, every meeting they attend, every company event or training they're supposed to be attending, including bathroom and snack breaks or lunches.

The importance of the PAWS in calculating the Asshole Density Ratio can now be discussed.

A Quick Measure of Dysfunctionality: The Asshole Density Ratio (ADR)

A good rule of thumb to measure the dysfunctionality of a company is the **Asshole Density Ratio (ADR)**. The ADR is a quick way to determine the level of dysfunctionality of a company. Companies with higher ADRs tend to be more dysfunctional. Those with lower ADRs less so. The ADR is just another ratio among the metrics used to measure the company's performance.

The ADR can be easily calculated by dividing the number of assholes within a given space at the company by the total number of employees in that same space converted into a percentage. There is an Executive Supplement Factor (ESF) for executives, or other high-level directors and managers, who may not reside in the space being sampled but must be included to make the calculation accurate.

The following is the formula for the ADR:

$$ADR = \frac{(Assholes\ in\ Test\ Space)}{(Employees\ in\ Test\ Space + ESF)} \times 100$$

The employee calculating their company's ADR starts by taking exactly a hundred steps in all four directions from their work area or, again, in dysfunctional parlance, the PAWS. As was just shown, the PAWS is the key building block of the dysfunctional company and required for calculating the ADR. It's the home base, or starting point, from where the ADR is measured.

If the employee's work station is less than a hundred steps from a wall or a window, or other obstacle, he or she should compensate by taking steps in an alternate direction, until the total number of steps is a hundred. This will guarantee the employee has a sufficient sample of his or her coworkers for counting assholes.

However, it can't be overstated, managers and executives still need to be factored in for a complete and accurate calculation of the ratio.

If there are executives or managers within the test square, they can be included in the calculation. The ESF isn't necessary. If not, as is often the case in the dysfunctional company, where the nobility and aristocrats are physically separated (on different floors or buildings, or in concrete bunkers offsite) from the serfs and peasants, a sample of higher-ranking staff must be thrown in the mix to ensure a complete ratio.

What about remote employees? If they walk a hundred steps they may end up in the backyard or fall off a balcony. If they work at a coffee shop, or other publicly shared space, for example, they may bother innocent bystanders. How do they count the assholes in their company?

Simple. A square should be drawn around the icons representing as many of their coworkers as possible from the messaging application on the desktop of their laptop. Again, the ESF must be considered. If no executives or managers appear on the screen, just add some in to even out the ratio. Once the sample is complete, then the remote employee can proceed to calculate the ratio as explained above.

Companies with low ADRs, say, in the ten to twenty percent range, still have enough control, at this point, of their asshole impulses and keep on functioning. Once the ADR hits fifty percent, things start getting dicey. There may be good days, when things get done, and bad days, where they don't. Some conflict between people at the company is inevitable.

Over seventy percent, the company is clearly in the red zone and is being run by assholes. Combined with asshole employees, this is a lethal combination. Conflicts are frequent, cooperation low and tension high – the perfect ingredients for company stagnation. Inertia is key here.

A Word About Outside Boards of Directors

CEOs don't drop from the sky. Some CEOs think they were sent from heaven as God's Gift (see Habit Seven for an explanation) to the dysfunctional company. Unless the CEO is the founder of the company and, obviously, self-appointed, CEOs are appointed by an outside board of directors or group of investors. In the case of a partnership, a common structure in professional service companies, they may be elected by a group of partners.

Even self-appointed CEO founders may eventually have to create an outside board as their company grows.

Either way, outside boards and overseeing investors aren't involved in the management or daily operations of their companies. The focus of this book is on the daily confusion and mismanagement of the dysfunctional company.

Though there are boards comprised of nincompoops from other dysfunctional companies who spread their incompetence to the board they serve, they're not involved enough in the daily mismanagement to be covered in this book.

Then, again, there are also boards whose members may have considerable business acumen and strategy chops. Of course, these people are either not overseeing a dysfunctional company, or are trying to turn one around, and wouldn't be a focus of this book either.

How to Use This Book to Screw Up Your Business

The first step in creating a dysfunctional company is outlined in Habit One. This habit must be mastered first before proceeding on to the next habits. After successful completion of the first habit, the remaining habits can be completed in any order.

Another way to effectively use this book is to rip it up and throw it in the air. The chapters falling on the floor can be picked up at random and shuffled like a bunch of playing cards. At this point, to avoid bankruptcy later, the book can simply be tossed in the garbage right now and no further action is required.

On the other hand, if the brain surgeons at the dysfunctional company want to continue playing the card game, usually the case at companies with no vision or self-awareness, they can follow the habits in any order. The endgame is always the same, in any case – a totally dysfunctional company – no matter how the card game is played.

What's Next?

This little book will guide those intent on wrecking their company. It's a roadmap for company destruction. Following the suggestions in this book will lead to disaster. It will slow down and damage the business, if not put the company out of business altogether.

The dysfunctional company isn't in the business of doing business. It's in the business of bureaucracy and creating people problems. The dysfunctional company has twin enemies: its employees and its customers. The first step in the journey of a thousand miles to company destruction begins next with Habit One.

> **Twin enemies of the dysfunctional company:**
> 1) **Its employees**
> 2) **Its customers**

Habit One:
If It Makes Sense, Don't Do It

"Our strategy is just to lay off people every quarter when sales go down."

Habit One:
If It Makes Sense, Don't Do It

"We can't do that. That's too easy. It would make sense."

The simplest most obvious way to get anything done should always be avoided. The simplest question must always have a complicated answer. The simplest request, no matter how small, should be an adventure down a path of bureaucratic torture and aggravation – endless approvals, tons of paperwork, and non-stop meetings – and, of course, the ubiquitous e-mail chain, the backup, known as, "the paper trail."

Take sticky notes, for example. It should be easier to leave the office and go down the street to a stationery store to buy sticky notes than to go through purchasing.

Why sticky notes? Sticky notes are the glue holding the dysfunctional company together. They're a vital part of every employee's nightmarish daily routine, as discussed in Habit Six about abuse of employees.

Going through purchasing means filling out a form for a request. There's nothing odd about request forms. Every company has to keep track of its purchases and inventory of office supplies. In the dysfunctional company, it's not that easy. The request form is just the beginning of a series – not just one – of approvals, maybe even a meeting of managers, or even – the dreaded – cascade of e-mails.

The anxious employee could starve to death, or pass out, if they hold their breath, waiting for their sticky notes. If they go the unconventional route – trying to buy them on their own – then they would have to file an expense report. That would be Act II of the dysfunctional drama, called "Dealing with Purchasing, An Office Tragedy."

This is just office supplies. The same nonsense, on an even bigger scale, plays out for projects. Taken to a higher level, imagine trying to change company policy, or strategy. The fun is only beginning. The paths required to go through the company maze are mind boggling. Combined with a toxic work environment (reflected in a high ADR) and managers and employees at each other's throats, it doesn't get any better.

The standard operating procedure for the dysfunctional company is for every action, and every decision, to be based on power, politics, and ego. Competence, knowledge, and expertise should never be considered in any decision. The needs of the bureaucracy must come before the needs of the business and, of course, before common sense. Office politics rules.

> **The dysfunctional company obeys**
> **The Laws of Physics:**
> **For every attempt at action, there is an equal**
> **and opposite bureaucratic counterreaction.**

This is the principal habit from which all the habits are derived. This habit must be mastered thoroughly before moving on to the other habits. Its brilliance is in its elegance and simplicity. Its transformational power is its ability to turn a perfectly functioning profitable company into a dysfunctional babbling mess.

It's guaranteed to lower profits, decrease productivity, lower employee morale, create dissension in the ranks, encourage executive greed and management indifference, inhibit growth and stifle innovation – all ingredients of the successful dysfunctional company.

> **Habit One has also been known as:**
> **1) If It Doesn't Work, Keep Doing It**
> **2) If It's Simple, Make It Complicated**

This is everywhere, every day, In the dysfunctional company. It's part of the fun that makes life interesting at the company and keeps everybody on their toes. Never a dull moment in the insane asylum mistaken as a working company.

The Principle of the Appearance of Activity

The dysfunctional company is a beehive of activity. People running around, papers flying everywhere, phones and mobiles ringing, computer screens blinking. Conference rooms are full of people in meetings, some of them there for days without food and water. Groups of people move around in packs, supposedly from the same work group, talking excitedly about their latest project, or more likely, their latest golf game or sexual escapade.

For remote employees, the beehive is virtual. It's on their laptop screens. Windows popping in and out, flashing icons buzzing across the screen, chat rooms ablaze with conversation, and then there's e-mail. Tons of messages flashing at the speed of light on top of the other open windows. Alerts should be constantly flashing to disrupt any productive work the employee is trying to do.

Getting work done? That's impossible at the dysfunctional company. Anything that distracts employees is fair game at the dysfunctional company. Barriers should be erected and, if they're not high enough, make them higher.

There are too many other fires to put out, too much bureaucratic nonsense to chase, before any attention can be turned to real work. There are e-mails to answer, meetings to attend, unnecessary extra training, reports and more reports to fill out. There are multiple e-mails with requests for the same thing from different departments – departments that don't communication with each other. On top of that, there may be IT outages or forced socializing out of the blue at any moment to ruin the day.

Little do employees know, dark forces under the surface are working to prevent their projects from getting done, let alone even getting started. The typical day is an obstacle course of activities meant to wear the employee down.

This is **The Principle of the Appearance of Activity** in action. There is a lot of activity. But how much of that activity is really productive work?

The Principle of the Appearance of Activity:
A lot of visible activity, no results
A lot of motion, no productive work

But then, what is productive work?

What is Productive Work?

Productive work consists of three things:

1. Producing and selling a product or service.
2. Providing service to customers after the sale.
3. Developing or improving the product or service.

It sounds obvious, doesn't it? Not so in the dysfunctional company. If it makes sense, don't do it. Every obstacle should be put in the way of getting anything done, especially productive work. Whether being tied up by e-mails or in meetings, employees should be distracted by nonsense and company procedures.

If it makes sense to handle something minor with one simple e-mail, don't do it. Have a meeting. Better yet, go for broke. Have a series of meetings. Why not? One meeting just doesn't do the trick in the dysfunctional company.

Take something simple like adding a column to a spreadsheet. Even this routine activity should require approval. Better to waste time in a meeting, or meetings, than just add the damn column, even if it could have been discussed in a single phone call or e-mail. Maybe include IT in the meeting, since office software is involved. Maybe include other stakeholders, even ones not involved in the project. Who knows? The more the merrier is the watchword at the dysfunctional company. The more irrelevant the stakeholder, the better. The options to slow things down are endless.

With all the e-mails back and forth, followed by pointless meetings and approvals, five minutes to add a column to a spreadsheet can be turned into a two-day bureaucratic logjam.

People need to be tied up as much as possible, all day, if necessary, in the pursuit of company inertia. The day should be filled with fighting bureaucratic battles and putting out fires with customers, instead of any meaningful work. Since most of the products and services the dysfunctional company produces are crap, any ways, fighting with angry customers is just another day at the office.

As sworn enemies of the dysfunctional company, customers are particularly singled out for abuse. The poor treatment of customers is discussed in Habit Five about the key role of hostile – or phantom – Customer Disservice departments.

The powers that be at the dysfunctional company are the biggest consumers of management fads. They scour bookshelves for recent business books. Every new management fad, especially if it has some fancy scientific-sounding name, which only a PhD would understand, should be implemented. No thought should be given to whether the fad would actually work at the company. That would make sense. The dysfunctional company loves to brag it's implementing the latest thing, and then hides the fact that it isn't working at all.

Every rule and procedure should be followed to the letter, especially if it obstructs work and stifles innovation.

No battle is too small in the war against employees and customers.

The Three Levels of Inertia

Bureaucratic stonewalling and nonsensical activity result in poor productivity at three levels in the dysfunctional company: daily activities, project management and overall strategy.

Daily activities are one-off items needed to get the bureaucratic machinery in gear. These are simple requests for getting office supplies, filling out forms for approvals, such as for expenses and travel, filling out time sheets and reports, and requesting training. It could also include expensive or complex items, like getting laptops or company cell phones. Many of these requests, initially, can be done online on the company internal web site without having to interact or call any other employee directly.

More likely, in the dysfunctional company, there will be a snag, even for little items. Someone will have to call someone, a lunch will need to be scheduled to discuss the matter, or a political favor given to move the bureaucratic mountain. Some annoying person will have to deal with another annoying person higher up.

Whatever it is, something will go wrong and the Gods of the Hierarchy must be appeased.

That's just to get sticky notes. Imagine trying to promote a good idea that would help the business. Forget it. Every request must start with some sort of required paperwork or form sent to the employee's supervisor. That request may then move on to that supervisor's supervisor, and then maybe to the next supervisor, and so on up the chain, all the way up to where the air gets thin in the office. Nosebleeds at high altitudes are common for executives at dysfunctional companies hiding atop ivory towers.

In any case, back to the initial paperwork that started this bureaucratic escapade. The paperwork should beget a meeting. Maybe not just any meeting, but an "exploratory committee" to determine if more meetings are necessary or, maybe even, a permanent standing committee.

Every meeting should beget another meeting, and then another, and so on ad infinitum.

It would make sense to have someone who understands the issue at hand, and knows what they're doing, to run a meeting or committee. Instead, the wrong people should always be chosen to run meetings and committees. The boss's pet rather than someone competent should be put in charge. This includes the usual cast of know-it-alls and ego-maniacs who staff the dysfunctional company. Once the wrong person is in charge, it's a given everything will run off the rails.

Committees have a life of their own. They spawn subcommittees, which spawn more meetings, more reports, more discussions and maybe even a whole new department of useless activity. This is the bureaucrat's dream: their own department with regular, usually weekly, project meetings. Orphaned and rogue departments with no purpose are common at dysfunctional companies.

The subcommittees then create their own so-called working groups, a code name for another subcommittee, sucking in more employees in the process. These working groups can refer issues to other committees, other departments, requiring more resources and, of course, more approvals into a daisy chain of gridlock. Layers are built upon layers, like a top-heavy wedding cake about to tip over.

Ultimately, nothing gets done. Those sticky notes never arrive. The big idea gets lost in a rabbit hole never to be seen again. The regular meetings descend into darkness. Everything gets tied up, needs more approvals, another report, more reviews, more meetings, more discussions, more e-mails, more phone calls. No one knows what to do. The landscape keeps changing.

So, what do they do? They call another meeting.

Regular Gridlock:
The Vital Role of The Weekly Meeting (TWM)

The skilled bureaucrat knows how to stall progress at the last minute, just as a request is approaching the finish line. If it looks promising, it must be a mirage. The bureaucratic cook always throws more spice into the stew: one more approval, one more meeting, one more committee, one more study until the request falls into a black hole, never to be seen or heard of again. In between, there is a blizzard of e-mails. There must be a paper trail. Someone will have to explain why something didn't get done.

The goal should be to schedule permanent meetings. The ultimate type of permanent meeting is **The Weekly Meeting (TWM,** pronounced "tweem"). TWMs should be etched on every employee calendar like epithets on a tombstone. They're purpose is to maim and kill.

Employees attending excessive TWMs suffer from emotional disorders, or break out in hives and rashes. Insomnia and night sweats are also common in TWM sufferers. Just thinking about the next TWM is enough to make even the healthiest of employees nauseous. Some have even dropped dead prematurely, either during or just after the meeting.

TWMs are one of the best time sucks in the dysfunctional toolkit. If it makes sense to cancel a TWM when there is no new information, the TWM must still be held, under Habit One. An empty TWM, where participants are staring at each other, or talking about their kids and pets, is preferable to not holding a meeting.

TWMs should have precedence over every other meeting. TWMs are the king of meetings. Employees can use them as an excuse to bump other meetings. "I can't attend that meeting. I have a TWM," or "I'm already triple-booked," the overbooked employee will say.

Meeting Hell is such a fundamental pillar of the dysfunctional company, it has its own Habit – Habit Four.

If a simple request can't get handled, imagine trying to get a whole project done. Projects are a landmine of requests, meetings and approvals, enough to keep even the hungriest of bureaucrats salivating.

If all else fails, create a spreadsheet. This itself will require more e-mails that could blossom into a full-blown meeting situation. It doesn't make sense, so it must be done.

Auditors and Lawyers: The Company Bouncers

Even better, call in the shock troops. The legal and audit departments are the bouncers of the dysfunctional company. They can be counted on to keep employees from doing their jobs. Their motto: "The answer is 'no'. What's the question?" Every rule must be followed to the letter, even if it holds up the business, even if it no longer makes sense. No rule is too small.

In well-run companies, lawyers and auditors support the business. Lawyers keep the company out of legal trouble – a tall order in the unethical dysfunctional company – and auditors make sure the company meets regulatory compliance – another tall order in the disorganized dysfunctional company. Auditors may also make sure the company meets internal standards for financial reporting, IT standards and security, for example.

Not so in the dysfunctional company, where they're **Occasional Business Blockers (OBB,** pronounced "Oh, Bob," emphasis on the "Oh"). Lawyers and auditors come out of the woodwork when least expected, summoning employees at will into poorly lit conference rooms, strapping them into chairs and asking uncomfortable questions about personal hygiene or minor items in expense reports, like sticky notes.

They fire questions rapidly at the employee until he or she cries, or just submits from exhaustion and signs a confession. Some employees have been known to break out in a cold sweat during interrogation sessions.

Auditors in the dysfunctional company should be a feared secret police unit. They look for minor infractions of every company rule, no matter how insignificant. They attend meetings under cover. They mingle with employees in the company cafeteria, looking warily at all passersby. They roam freely around the office in small groups, like street gangs, going up and down aisles, looking at paperwork, or laptop screens, on employee desks.

Some auditors have tattoos with gang signs and spiked hair to look more intimidating. Some wear mirrored sunglasses. Others wear t-shirts with slogans, like: "Hell can wait. We're here to intimidate," or "The gig is up. You've been caught violating policy." They even have secret handshakes and hand signals, so employees won't know what they're doing.

Once auditors arrive, they first tell the alleged offender to step back from their desk and put their hands on their lap. They encircle the employee and flash business cards in their face. They may introduce themselves with euphemistic titles like "Internal Control," or "Inspector." Whatever they call themselves, they're still auditors.

Employees who violate even minor policies have been known to disappear in the middle of the night, snatched away secretly from their PAWS and taken for months at a time to company correction camps, also known as "company training."

Remote employees can't escape the reach – or the wrath – of auditors and lawyers either. An icon, permanently embedded on their computer screen, with the image of a goon wearing sunglasses staring at them is a sign they're being watched. Auditors should keep remote employees under constant surveillance. Out of sight and out of mind, remote employees are under more suspicion than their office-based colleagues, since auditors can't see their transgressions directly.

Lawyers in the dysfunctional company will do what they do best – threaten to file lawsuits. They start their assault with warning letters written in a language nobody at the company understands. The dysfunctional company attorneys will say, "It can't be done," even if it's an innovative idea benefitting the business.

If the lawyers and auditors can't screw things up, it's time to call in outside business wreckers: the consultants and investors.

White Knights and Consultants: Saviors or Destroyers?

Sometimes, it makes sense for a functioning company to reach out for assistance – to consultants with expertise in their field for fresh ideas, or to investors when a growing business needs to expand.

Instead, consultants are weapons in the dysfunctional company arsenal for fighting political battles. Heavily armed with supercharged laptops and spreadsheets, consultants can be easily spotted in the office, wearing tin-foil helmets with tall antennas. The antennas receive the latest business and management bullshit ideas from outer space, or maybe just from business school gobbledygook.

On the surface, consultants may sound hip and cool and even intelligent. They're really only spouting the latest management mumbo jumbo from recent business best sellers any idiot can pick up in a bookstore. They write fancy reports on designer stationery suitable for use later as toilet paper in the company bathroom. They put together neat PowerPoint presentations and then walk away before the damage they present is implemented.

Consulting companies themselves are sometimes dysfunctional. They have to make their daily bread, as well, and should bill as many hours as possible to soak the client. They should always book more hours than there are in the day. If there are only 40 hours in a work week, they should book, say, 120 hours for that week, based on the consultant's clock of 24 hours of work each business day.

In addition, rather than telling the client the truth, which would probably be too painful anyways, they should tell the client what they want to hear. A naysayer consultant won't get the repeat business needed to keep their overbilling pipeline flowing.

Consultants are at the top of the food chain of sycophant hangers-on to the dysfunctional company. Their goal is to keep leeching off the dysfunctional company, as long as possible, convincing them it needs their services to function.

Consultants are staffed with MBAs, which stands for Masters of Bureaucratic Administration. MBAs learn very little in school applicable to the upside-down world of the dysfunctional company. They review case studies for companies with some hope of being turned around, rarely encountering truly toxic companies whose turf battles and bureaucracy are legendary.

Make no mistake. Consultants are out for blood. They're the drivers in the cars of the company demolition derby. They smash up departments and injure their annoying employees. It's much easier to let an outsider do the dirty work, than for the dysfunctional company to take responsibility for mass layoffs.

Outside investors are the other weapon of choice for the dysfunctional company. If consultants are the demolition derby, outside investors are the wrecking ball sent to finish the job. They're the company equivalent of the repo man who comes to take the property back after foreclosure.

They pose as White Knights in shining armor on high horses, swords held high. They claim to be rescuing the company through acquisition or with fresh infusions of capital. Instead, in the dysfunctional company, they leave a path of destruction.

The White Knights bring in their own people, pushing aside experienced employees, some of whom may have been at the company for years and know all the ins and outs better than the invading crusaders. If the White Knights are also from dysfunctional companies, they would never consider whether the departments, or functions, between the acquiring and the acquired company would be compatible.

Battle plans for the acquisition were probably drawn up in smoke-filled secret rooms or poorly lit underground bunkers by people, wearing black gloves, probably investment bankers, carrying swagger sticks and wearing eye patches. They come bearing briefcases, or more likely laptops, with spreadsheets. The only thing they did, before planning their attack, was to pour over numbers projected on screens. They never thought about how the merged companies would work together.

If there are incompatible IT systems, or contradictory marketing approaches, or different accounting systems, maybe different logistics systems, maybe different manufacturing processes, or even different office cultures, to name a few examples, who cares? Not the White Knights.

As usually happens in dysfunctional companies, it's all about the numbers. It's all about the money. They're only about lining their pockets and squeezing as much money out of the deal as possible. Does the merger make sense from a strategic perspective? Who knows? Not the White Knights. As will be seen shortly, the dysfunctional company has no strategy. They flip and they flop from one stupid idea to the next. So, they have no idea whether the deal is a good for the company or not.

It would make sense for an outside CEO brought in as a White Knight to be paid for performance. If the company does well, the new CEO would be compensated appropriately. If not, the CEO's failure would be reflected in his or her compensation. Their bonus for restructuring the company should be paid like a sales commission. If they turn around the sinking ship, they get paid. If it sinks, they don't. They drown with it.

Instead, the dysfunctional company lets the White Knight loot and pillage at will. They run the dysfunctional company into the ground, chop it up with their swords and then are let go themselves, only to be rewarded with an obscene bonus package – a so-called "golden parachute."

This is just another example of, "If it makes sense, don't do it."

In the meantime, they leave a trail of misery in their wake through mass layoffs and shattered work lives. Sure, there really may be duplication of staff or departments in a merged company. The White Knight buzzword is "redundant." White Knights don't see it that way. Anything in their path, anything in their way, could be called "redundant" as an excuse to shed blood in the halls.

Employees Need to Be Aware: The Proper Use of Crap Detectors

Employees need to watch these company dramas carefully. They need crap detectors strapped to their belts that flash when company bullshit is flying around. In many cases, the problem, particularly in the dysfunctional company, is the devices are always going off. This makes it difficult for employees to distinguish between real crap and office gossip and rumors. Whatever their crap detectors say, employees still need to be on the lookout for signs of outside troublemakers.

If they spot outsiders wearing tin-foil helmets, horse-mounted knights in shining armor in the hall or – remote employees should pay special attention – on their Zoom or chat applications, they should know it's time to pack up their toys and move on to the next dysfunctional gig.

Either way, whether through death by consultant or murder by White Knights, the dysfunctional company employee should keep up their guard and prepare their resume. In fact, it's a good idea for employees to always have an up-to-date resume handy. In the chaos and confusion of the dysfunctional company, employees never know whether today will be their last. Employees are the last to know. It's always a surprise. The company Angel of Death never comes announced.

All companies, functional and dysfunctional, run into business challenges. Even well-run companies aren't immune from business shocks. Inevitably, there will be unexpected competition or weak sales. Maybe the way the product or service is delivered needs to be updated. Maybe marketing needs a face lift. Maybe factors outside the company's control impact the product or service – the impact of new regulations or legal issues, or the economy going south.

There are times when reorganization or layoffs are necessary to save the company. There are times when the company may have to take a step back and recalibrate its plans and strategies.

It's never easy for any company, well-managed or not, to go through these periods. The leaders of functional companies know how to restrain their dictatorial impulses for the good of the company. They plan for contingencies. They think ahead.

They try their best, though it doesn't always work, to prepare for disasters. They map out worst-case scenarios, even if it's painful or uncomfortable for management to think about. They know how to put their ego aside and look in the mirror, even if what they see is ugly. They don't make excuses. They take ownership. They solve problems. They don't look for someone, or something, to blame.

Yet, as they say, even in functional companies, the best laid plans can go awry. Not so in the dysfunctional company. They make it worse. They don't even have plans – that would make sense and must be avoided – or strategies and contingencies or backups to screw up. The only backups are in the toilets in the company bathrooms, even that they can't fix, since it would take too much paperwork, too many signatures or maybe a bathroom review meeting. Even more nonsensical, create a mysterious TWM and call it the **Standing Lavatory Observation Committee**

(**SLOC**, pronounced "slock" to rhyme with "schlock").

The dysfunctional company is so tied up in knots internally with people problems and stifling business processes that it can't innovate and change course. Internal communication is so poor, as will be discussed in detail in Habit Three, it can't even see problems coming, let alone communicate solutions, until it's too late.

Our Strategy is Fancy Company Events

It would make sense to have a strategy or a plan. The dysfunctional company has neither. It has fancy company events with dancing bears and sword swallowers. The flashier, the better. Fireworks and celebrity performances are de rigueur. Watching cheerleaders with fancy costumes and sparklers dance and sing is more fun than writing boring business plans.

Writing a business plan? That would make sense, which, of course, isn't how the dysfunctional company operates. It would take too much work, and too many meetings and e-mails.

Who needs a strategy when you can be entertained? The dysfunctional company is a master at setting up cool events in fancy hotels and exotic resorts to get everybody excited, or maybe just wasted – from executives and management down to employees and maintenance staff.

At most company events, executives and department heads are supposed to do their dog and pony show between the circus events. They may talk about exciting new product or service roll outs, or the rosy future of the company. Then they end up talking about a utopia that totally misrepresents reality at the dysfunctional company.

Too often, at the dysfunctional company, these events are just an excuse to get out of the office or, for remote employees, get out of the house, and party. They're a company version of Spring Break. They're only about excessive drinking, or other bad behavior, on the company tab in the name of team "bonding.".

Everybody leaves these events feeling good – even if still sober – or, at least, weighted down with bags of company-branded swag – more junk to put on their already crowded desktops.

They may even learn about other non-functioning departments showcasing their supposed activities with slick presentation. It may also be an opportunity to network and build relationships. These friendships are short-lived, since after the event, everybody goes back to their business-as-usual confrontational stance. Company tribes are hard to break up, even at feel-good events.

Feel-good events aren't the only distractions from strategy at the dysfunctional company. The dysfunctional company mistakes benchmarks and sale targets for strategy. These are goals, not strategy.

Strategy isn't cool slogans either. They dysfunctional company loves to hang banners around the office, or put them on laptop screen savers: "We're the best!" "We always win!" "We met our goals this year!" or "Our department is better than your department!" Here's a gem for dealing with the competition: "Our screwed-up company can beat up your screwed-up company."

Employees will be expected to stand up at meetings during pre-arranged intervals and put their hand over their chest and parrot these cool slogans in unison, and then sit down and continue their meeting.

Another motivational slogan for encouraging salespeople is: "The beatings will stop when sales improve." The philosophy of "Let's keep beating up salespeople by always raising their targets until it's unrealistic" is only a sound strategy at the dysfunctional company.

Setting goals, or creating benchmarks, are worthwhile activities. They're only part of a comprehensive strategy, not the strategy itself. The organization must also be structured around execution of a strategy, something iffy in the dysfunctional company with its rigid hierarchies and battling departments.

Strategy is a competitive analysis of a company's strengths and weaknesses and what differentiates it in the marketplace. It's about how the company competes against its rivals. It's about its competitive advantage over others in its field. It's about its core competency.

Core competencies are an oxymoron in the dysfunctional company. Like the company's daily actions, they make no sense. They have neither a core nor a competency. The dysfunctional company is never really sure what it's good at or, for that matter, what it should be doing. It flounders around and flips and flops like a fish out of water from one business fad to another. It does what doesn't make sense. It trips over itself and can't innovate. It can't keep up with the times and eventually becomes obsolete.

It takes meaningful work, which the dysfunctional company is incapable of doing, to build plans and strategy. When things break down, as they always do, there is always scapegoating.

Scapegoating is Part of Our Business Process

The Blame Game is big at the dysfunctional company. Nobody should ever take responsibility, at any level, from the top down, for what goes wrong at the dysfunctional company.

It's always somebody else's fault. Some people at the dysfunctional company have stiff knuckles from finger pointing all the time.

In dysfunctional companies, some problems are systemic and not the fault of one individual. It would make sense to review the root cause of a problem. It can't be overemphasized: If it makes sense don't do it. It's much easier to blame an individual than to solve a problem. Witch hunts are common, often daily occurrences, at the dysfunctional company.

Employees who are victims of company witch hunts should be tied by their wrists to a food cart and dragged through the halls of the office in a public spectacle – sort of like watching a public hanging in the town square. These events should be recorded and the videos shown on an internal company web site, available to both office-bound and remote employees.

When remote employees are the target of a witch hunt, they should be publicly shamed by videos posted of them doing something embarrassing at a forced social event, especially if it involves alcohol or nudity.

Videos should be captioned with the employee's alleged offense, like "This single employee is responsible for all of the decline in sales last year," or "This employee caused our stock price to go down last quarter," or "This employee is anti-social and doesn't drink enough at company events."

Posters should be put up on the walls in the office, and posted online, with a picture of the offending employee that can be defaced with black markers. There is nothing that strikes more fear in a recalcitrant employee than to see devil horns and goatees painted on their pictures. This is the company equivalent of the scarlet letter, though adultery might, or might not, be the issue.

The targeted employee should be made to feel they're the root of all evil at the dysfunctional company.

Humiliating employees in public will remind them that no one is safe at the dysfunctional company.

Anyone can be blamed, at any time, at any level, from the CEO on down to the basement, for any problem at the company.

Stupidity, Stupidity Everywhere and Not a Drop of Brains

The dysfunctional company is full of examples of simple things handled stupidly every day. These range from screwed up orders for laptops and software, and lost expense reports or requests for time off to biggies like poor policies, weak or non-existent strategies and the wrong employees assigned to projects.

The dysfunctional company mistakenly calls time off "Mental Health Days," which doesn't make sense, since it would take more than a day in rehab for most employees to recover from the trauma of working at the dysfunctional company.

It would make sense to keep a popular feature in a product. Instead, the dysfunctional company suddenly removes features and changes services without notice. The thought of notifying customers – or heaven forbid, asking their opinion – of changes to their products and services is an afterthought. Customers are a nuisance anyways (see Habit Five about Customer Disservice), and their suggestions should be ignored.

Removing features and services are a good way for the dysfunctional company to cut costs and skimp on service. Improving the product or service for the customer is never a good idea.

If the dysfunctional company is providing a 24x7 service, customers should never be informed about planned outages. It's better to let outraged customers swamp Customer Disservice with calls or e-mails, which can be dodged through automated systems, or disconnected altogether, than to provide the service as promised on time. The same goes for unplanned service failures. Keep the customers in the dark until they complain, and then ignore their inquiries.

The customer is never right. The customer never comes first. The customer should be screwed every which way they turn. This is the heart of Habit One.

It would make sense to locate the office near employees. Instead, the dysfunctional company puts its offices near the CEO and executives, who live in unaffordable neighborhoods far from employees. It's better to have employees commute long hours hoping they arrive fresh in the office after fighting traffic, then to have the office in a convenient location. Long and stress-filled commutes are the perfect prescription for chipper and crisp employees.

Another great reason to locate the office far from employees is to force them to work remotely, and then tell them later – usually through a mass e-mail campaign – they have to come back to the office to keep their jobs.

If it makes sense to let employees work remotely, bring them back into the office. Employees can't be trusted, especially if they're out of sight of the heavily armed goons in the watchtowers overlooking the PAWSs in the office.

It would make sense to keep employees with similar skills together. Instead, employees at the dysfunctional company should be spun around like on a merry-go-around. They need to be tossed around with frequent and unannounced reorgs. They shouldn't know from one day to the next who they report to, or to which work group they belong. Besides perpetual organizational reshuffling, where employees sit on any given day – aka, their PAWS – should be a mystery.

Employees with similar skills, like a group of software developers, an accounting team, or marketing for a product group, for example, are islands of expertise. If their group is lucky enough to not be blown to bits through random reorgs, they may still feel like islands of competence floating aimlessly amid a cesspool of management confusion and ignorance.

De-desking and office homelessness are a constant threat hanging over employees. More details about the gentle way facilities management should handle the location of employees in the office is covered in Habit Six. This should be foremost on the minds of remote employees, who might be rethinking returning to the office. Of course, they can be effectively de-desked from home, if they're called back involuntarily to the office.

As for laptops, computer equipment and software needed from IT to get work done, forget it. They're stillborn in purchasing before a bureaucrat can even say "no". Typical responses might be: "It's not in this year's budget." "Maybe next year." "Maybe when Hell freezes over." And then the ultimate kicker: "I don't have authority." Even if an employee gets what they need from IT, getting it set up and working with the Helpless Desk is another bureaucratic boondoggle.

The Lords of IT and the tremendous power they have over employees in the dysfunctional company are discussed in detail in Habit Two about turf battles.

Office furniture has been known to disappear in sink holes, never to reach intended recipients. Screwed up red tape, wrong approvals, trucks lost in dark alleys, poorly stocked warehouses, misdirected deliveries – then sending cryptic e-mails with weird excuses. This is the dysfunctional company at its best.

Employees standing around by their desks and workstations waiting for chairs that never arrive is another sign of a dysfunctional company. This shouldn't be confused with other reasons employees may be standing around. Since unproductive activity is a hallmark of the dysfunctional company, employees standing around doing nothing is a common sight. This is one exception to the Principle of the Appearance of Activity.

Some employees standing around may just be engaging in Unproductive Social Activities (USA). Many have been given unclear or unrealistic work assignments and just throw up their hands and walk around. Their management is clueless and can't help them either, or will punish them for asking too many questions. Competent people asking for direction from morons is forbidden at the dysfunctional company. It never ends well.

Other employees maybe standing to pay their respects to co-workers who have dropped dead at their desks. As explained fully in Habit Six, dead employees should be left at their desk as employee idols and office heroes. They're role-models for the living dead already walking the office with a dazed look, or remote employees staring blankly at their screens with glassy eyes.

Another sure sign of the correct implementation of Habit One is the expulsion of the Visionary Founder. Few companies start off as dysfunctional. Many started with an entrepreneurial founder with a great idea. Sometimes they take off and do fine. Others, who have mastered Habit One, eventually fall into dysfunctionality.

At that point, the Visionary Founder, who was competent and full of energy, gets crushed by his or her own creation. They couldn't even get a job at their own company. HR would screen them out in a flash.

That's only the beginning of the descent into chaos. The next step is turf battles, the next dysfunctional habit.

Habit Two:
Fighting Turf Battles Is Better Than Cooperating

"Our department can beat up your department."

Habit Two:
Fighting Turf Battles Is Better Than Cooperating

"I don't care if they're dead. I need more direct reports in my department."

The dysfunctional company is in a constant state of turmoil. It's at war with itself. Executives battling executives. Executives fighting their subordinates, then fighting vice presidents and directors. Vice presidents and directors, in turn, fighting each other, then fighting their direct reports, all the way down the feeding chain to managers and employees.

After managers receive their abuse from above, they turn around and immediately dish it out to their underlings. This creates an atmosphere of combative managers and belligerent employees, ready for bureaucratic knife fights in dark hallways over project assignments, staffing and budgeting.

The dysfunctional company is a textbook case of "The [*expletive deleted*] rolls downhill."

Turf battles are a natural for the dysfunctional company. A toxic culture combined with a high ADR are lethal ingredients. Turf battles are part of the company culture. It's just another day on the battlefield known as the dysfunctional office.

It's all about brute force and raw power. The dysfunctional company doesn't rely on the skills and brains, or even the expertise, for that matter, of its people. Instead, it's all about office politics and who has the most bureaucratic muscle.

The feudal lords at the dysfunctional company couldn't be bothered with running a business. They're too busy building their own little personal kingdoms and fiefdoms to be thinking about the good of the company.

The little warlords at the dysfunctional company use the following formula to build their internal armies:

Headcount = Power = Money

They think feathering their own nests gives them more power, more money, and a bigger slice of the pie. They think power translates into money. They couldn't be more wrong.

While they're building their forts, they're destroying the company from within. They're blocking progress and innovation, keeping the company from becoming a market leader. Meanwhile, more nimble competitors, with fewer castles and moats, are racing forward, stealing their customers, and improving the product and service, while the dysfunctional company is chasing its tail.

Teamwork? No way. It's not in the dysfunctional company's genes. It's every person for themselves. Everybody is grabbing at any available lifeboat to stay alive. The name of the game is Cover Your Ass. An ass uncovered is an ass out the door, thrown to the wolves, or laid off and thrown out in the cold. If it means stepping on someone's toes, or stabbing a teammate in the back, so be it.

Nobody wants to be another ghost with a resume looking for a job again in a world full of dysfunctional companies. The choices are stark. It's better to make it work, no matter how painful, right where you are. It's better to be in a bad relationship with some dysfunctional company than be alone without any dysfunctional company.

The dysfunctional company requires a structure to preserve both disharmony among its people and inertia in its activities. This is the pyramid with embedded silos.

The Optimal Dysfunctional Structure:
A Pyramid with Embedded Silos

The pyramid with embedded silos is the optimal form of organization for the dysfunctional company. The pyramid provides horizontal stratification and the silos divide the company along vertical lines. The silos are then embedded within the pyramid structure to create the right mix of dysfunctionality and roadblocks within the company.

Pyramids were commonly found in ancient civilizations around the world. Clearly, the dysfunctional company has its roots in antiquity. Just as the stones of the ancient pyramids are rigid and unchanged since antiquity, the organizational design of the dysfunctional company is often stuck in the past.

The structure of the organizational pyramid (see Figure 1) is identical to its physical counterpart with a triangular face from the side, and a square base that gets smaller as it goes up each level, until it reaches the peak at the top. Everyone's position in the pyramid indicates their rank within the organization. The more important their position, the higher their perch in the pyramid. For example, executives would be at the top, employees at the bottom, or base, with the rest of the different levels of management somewhere in between, depending on the dysfunctional company's hierarchy.

The Dysfunctional Pyramid

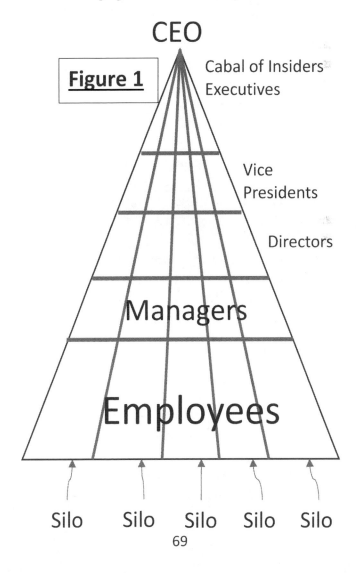

The dysfunctional pyramid has several layers, depending on the number of levels in the dysfunctional company's bureaucracy. The layers of the dysfunctional pyramid resemble a tiered wedding cake, except the little plastic figurine on top, instead of being a happy couple, is a single person with a hand outstretched, like a statue of a totalitarian dictator.

In the simplest example, the executives, which includes the Cabal of Insiders, resides at the top layer up to the summit. The Cabal of Insiders, as will be discussed shortly, is who really runs or, more accurately, mismanages the dysfunctional company. The CEO is always at the top, or peak, even if, in fact, he or she is just a powerless putz and leader in name only.

The next layers down in the pyramid contain a mishmash of lower-ranked executives, vice presidents and directors, depending on how the bureaucratic geniuses in the Cabal of Insiders have structured their direct reports and organizations. This is an optional layer, since in the dysfunctional company, these additional roles might just be absorbed by already overstretched executives above, or pushed below to already overburdened managers in the next layer down.

Regardless of the number of layers in the dysfunctional pyramid, the next level down would still be management, often just called "middle managers." In this model, the executive layer at the top is communicating directly with managers, rather than through other intermediaries, such as vice presidents or directors.

The managers, who are in the unenviable position of being sandwiched between demanding – and dictatorial – leadership above and just plain demanding employees below, are then tasked with passing the directives from above down to the next layer, the employees.

The rest of the company, meaning the remaining employees, are at the bottom layer of the pyramid, bearing the weight of the entire structure.

And then there are the silos . . .

Superimposed over the pyramid are vertical silos. Each silo stretches from the base all the way up to the peak. The silo is staffed from the bottom with a team of employees. It then runs up through layers of management, ending with a designated executive at its head. Each silo has its own set of employees, management and executive leader or sponsor.

Silos can be designed any number of ways in the dysfunctional company. They might represent a functional area, such as finance, marketing, IT, and so on, or they could be arranged by product lines, or even by geographical locations where facilities and staff are located.

Sometimes in the dysfunctional company, as would be expected under Habit One, the organization of silos is chaotic and makes no sense. Nobody really knows where they are, or where they belong in the company. Confusion about the organizational structure runs amok.

However silos are structured, the key thing is they need to be walled off from each other. They need to be hermetically sealed to prevent having direct bureaucratic contact. This keeps departments from communicating with each other and makes sure they work at cross purposes. The desired result is duplication of efforts and miscommunication. One silo won't know what the other is doing, allowing both to waste time and resources on identical projects.

Better yet, if the two projects are incompatible, the silo system will keep peace in the office, at least temporarily, since the dueling project teams and managers aren't even aware of each other. As usually happens, some joker from one silo will spill the beans in an underground communication channel, like a bathroom or breakroom (more about covert communication next in Habit Three), and then the opposing silos will know something is up and can face off.

Once word reaches both silos, their representatives will suit up for battle and rumble in the parking lot, throwing laptops and white boards at each other, while chanting company slogans. It isn't a pretty sight.

Silos also result in employees being harassed throughout the day for the same request from different departments. This is the silo system in action, where silos don't know what stuff they each have and are forced to reach out individually to already besieged employees for the same information. This is another goal of the silo system: block communication between departments.

Communication in the silo must always be vertical and remain only within the silo. It would make sense to have silos talk to each other, and maybe even, heaven forbid, share information. Under Habit One, this is prohibited.

A single piece of information, or even a single request, must require approvals, as many as possible, including meetings and paperwork and a lot of e-mails, before being allowed to traverse a silo boundary into enemy territory. It would be too easy for two individuals to be allowed to just directly pass information or requests to each other.

Besides, cooperation might break down office barriers, stop turf battles and end the tyranny of office politics. It might improve organizational behavior. Unfortunately, in the dysfunctional company, it leads to leadership and management feeling threatened or, the unthinkable, their egos bruised.

Other Benefits of Pyramids

The pyramid is also perfect for breeding arrogance within the dysfunctional company. People at higher levels can be condescending to those in lower levels. Fear and suspicion are essential ingredients of the best turf battles. Bad attitudes among supervisors and humiliation of those below create the best environment for the dysfunctional company.

Where advanced degrees (doctors, lawyers, PhDs, CPAs and MBAs) are required for management levels and above, there are endless opportunities to make nasty comments to less-pedigreed employees down below. Bosses with degrees should constantly remind their employees that they're inferior. Employees should be told that their work is low-level and unimportant, even if it's technical enough to require specialized or advanced training outside of a degree program.

Degree snobs should tell lesser employees they're probably overpaid for their unimportant work, and that they should feel privileged just to be working alongside such brilliant specimens of humanity.

Degree snobs are, of course, also know-it-alls. They think their degree transforms them into instant experts on everything. Those without prior experience managing people, for example, suddenly become HR gurus. Those with no marketing experience suddenly are sales experts. Those who have never invested a dime, seem to be experts on investments and finance.

Management with degrees and lesser-educated employees cohabitating at the dysfunctional company just fuels the already combustible mix of competing personalities and ambitious power centers at all levels of the organization. Those with degrees, and those without, is just another fault line in the dysfunctional company's turf wars.

The biggest benefit of the pyramid organization is its contribution to increasing the dysfunctional company's ADR. Since there are fewer positions as one goes up the pyramid, there are fewer opportunities for those below to advance. There simply aren't enough open positions above to accommodate all those below seeking promotions.

This encourages back-stabbing and asshole-type behavior – resulting in an uptick in the ADR – among those competing for the limited number of positions at higher levels. To get ahead in the dysfunctional company, every employee knows they must have sharp elbows to push their colleagues aside and be prepared to be betray their co-workers and team mates on their way to the top. Machiavelli would be proud.

Ambitious employees can be spotted by the rear-view mirrors strapped to their shoulders to watch for back stabbers, who could be anywhere: at their PAWS, in a meeting, in the hallway or lurking in a breakroom or bathroom.

A deeper dive into the top layers of the pyramid,. starting with the Cabal of Insiders down to management, will reveal more about how each contributes to the turf battles endemic to the dysfunctional company.

The Cabal of Insiders

At the very top of the pyramid is the **Cabal of Insiders**. This is the center of all power in the dysfunctional company. This is the mountain from which all decisions come down. Snow-capped and isolated, only C-suite executives can reach its peak. Sitting unseen above the clouds, it's a mystery to all who look up from below.

Many lesser mortals in the dysfunctional company have perished attempting to pierce the clouds to scale the peak. Precious few arrived there through superior skills or brilliant insights. Maybe they were lucky enough to show profit and loss statements consistently in the black for the divisions they managed on their way up the ladder. Maybe they had a brilliant idea, engineered a strategic acquisition, or improved the product or service, which amazingly got noticed.

Maybe they just laid off the right number of people, claiming to trim fat, when they, not the employees they canned, in fact, are the real fat in the organization. They may have cut costs in the process yet somehow still missed the real dead weight leeching off the company – executives and management who may be incompetent, unproductive, useless, and redundant.

Most likely, in the dysfunctional company, they succeeded because they knew the right power games to play, had the right connections, and knew who to step on, and when, on their way to the top. They knew who to throw under the bus and who to elevate. They always knew the best forced socializing event to attend to kiss the right asses.

Maybe they were in the right place at the right time. Maybe they were in the management track for movers and shakers, or just backstabbed their way into an exclusive "executive training program." Maybe the bureaucratic stars were aligned, the clouds opened and the sky cleared, pulling them up from the depths of the hierarchy. Maybe they just knew how to manipulate their way up through power vacuums during reorganizations and mass layoffs.

Who knows? Sometimes in the dysfunctional company, it's anybody's guess how some dumbos broke into the upper echelons. Maybe somebody slept with somebody. HR dares to ask.

Whatever they were doing, they spent more time chasing the centers of power rather than chasing new customers or new business. Their hunger for personal power and ego gratification was greater than their drive to advance the company and its business.

The Cabal of Insiders generally consists of the CEO and his or her C-suite direct reports. The CEO generally heads the wrecking crew. This may not always be the case, depending on how the Cabal of Insiders is organized.

If the CEO has all hands on the steering wheel and is alert and involved, the C-suite may be united behind him or her. In this case, the Cabal of Insiders consists of the entire C-suite headed by the CEO. This is the simplest best-case scenario for a harmonious Cabal of Insiders with little intrigue. Bickering and arguing are kept to a minimum or, at least, an acceptable level, so the gang can pursue its self-serving policies unobstructed. Everybody knows what they can steal from the company and which pockets to line – their own.

Unity could be an illusion, however, if the CEO is an arrogant buffoon – a common problem at the dysfunctional company – who has strong-armed the executive team behind him. This is where the bullheaded CEO intimidates the entire C-suite into bowing down and kissing his or her ring. This requires the CEO to replace the best executives with his or her own personal pets and sycophants. This type of CEO only works well with loyal yes-people, because, well, the CEO is always right. This type of CEO needs constant emotional reinforcement and ego stroking.

Then there are exceptions, where the CEO isn't totally in charge of the Cabal, another possibility in the dysfunctional company. If the CEO is whacked out, or incompetent, or both – another common problem at the dysfunctional company – the C-suite may splinter into opposing cliques on its own.

On the other hand, if the CEO is shrewd and calculating, he or she may have more control, deliberately dividing the C-suite into antagonistic camps. This way the father-figure CEO can maintain control through sibling rivalry among his executive children.

In these situations, there are the **Ingroup** and the **Outgroup**. The actual Cabal of Insiders is the Ingroup. The rest of the C-suite then are the Outgroup. The Ingroup keeps power by undermining the Outgroup, using ruthless and unethical tactics that would make Machiavelli blush.

In particularly treacherous C-suites, where executives hide switch-blades behind their backs, there may be many Outgroups, all vying for attention. As a rule, the more fractured the Outgroup, the more dysfunctional the company. Throw in a clueless CEO, particularly a figurehead plucked from another dysfunctional company, who has no idea what is swirling around him or her, and the source of the dysfunction is obvious.

Even the Cabal of Insiders itself is rife with intrigue, setting the tone for the rest of the company. It's no mystery where the culture of turf battles starts.

In the dysfunctional company, it's never really clear what the Cabal of Insiders is doing. They have secret rituals behind closed doors. They may be burning incense or roasting marshmallows over a specially-made hot plate in the executive conference room. They could be sitting in a circle on the floor, while the CEO plays a guitar and everybody is singing, "We are the company."

In especially intimate C-suites, they may be standing barefoot and shoulder-to-shoulder around a conference room table, holding hands. Hidden from HR in secret meeting rooms, they may get away with all kinds of unapproved, or inappropriate, physical activities.

In more hip dysfunctional companies, they may pass around dope, only from a legal dispensary, of course. If there isn't a dispensary nearby, the Cabal of Insiders may resort to passing a pipe with a homemade brew of banana peels from the local grocery. Whatever they're smoking, it must be pretty strong stuff, since some of the ideas coming out of the dysfunctional executive suite are definitely from the fourth or fifth dimension.

And whatever they're doing, it's not for the benefit of the company. It's only in the Cabal's best interests, and the Cabal's interests are always self-serving. It's to divvy up the pie among themselves, leaving customers and employees with scraps, if anything, at all.

Nobody ever really knows. The Cabal is hidden. Its executive suite is in sound-proof bunkers. It follows its own rules. Everything it does is classified Top Secret Doo-doo.

In the dysfunctional company, the Cabal of Insiders is nothing more than a bunch of vultures circling around the carcass of their prey. The rest of the company, and definitely its customers, don't count. They're out of sight and out of mind to the cave dwellers in the executive ivory tower.

Managers: Real Bosses or Glorified Employees?

Managers hold an interesting position in the dysfunctional pyramid. They're smack in the middle between the leaders and the followers in the dysfunctional company. When they look up the pyramid, they see executives, or in some pyramids, a confusing array of upper management between them and executives. When they look down, they see employees.

Managers in the dysfunctional company fall into two categories. They're either conduits between the top and bottom layers of the pyramid, or they're an extension of the employee layer just below them. Their role is either intermediary bosses without power or glorified employees.

When managers are intermediary bosses, they're just a transmission belt between the top and the bottom. Their job is just to shovel crap from above and turn around and dump it on their subordinates, the employees. They may appear to their employees like real bosses with authority. In fact, they're just pseudo-bosses with limited power. Any power these managers have is illusory.

When they're glorified employees, they get stepped on just like the employees below them, as will be explained in Habit Six. They're the last to know anything, and then are expected to be the messengers of bad news. Then, not surprisingly, they get blamed for the consequences of poor decisions made above them. Just like the rest of employees, they're dispensable and can be kicked out at a moment's notice.

The Angel of Death doesn't pass over managers.

In well-run companies, managers have great potential to lead their team. If they rose through the ranks because of their expertise, they can be the go-to person for their team. They can provide needed advice from their knowledge and experience. They can be a guide. They can be someone the team looks up to for both technical and emotional support. They provide real leadership.

More often, in the dysfunctional company, they're an incompetent weenie appointed by some political hack in upper management to just babysit the team. They have no idea what the team really does and probably don't care. They usually don't even have the background and expertise either to run the team.

Whatever their true role in the dysfunctional company, the job of managers is to berate and belittle employees. The manager's creed: **"Spare the criticism and spoil the employee."** Managers should never, under any circumstance, praise employees. Employees are to be hounded and scolded at every opportunity, for even the slightest misdeed, actual or perceived.

Generally, managers in the dysfunctional company should only talk to their employees to criticize and harass them. Managers should never acknowledge an employee, either publicly or privately, for a good job.

It's part of the manager's job to put employees in their place and show them who is boss. Their job is to make employees feel unimportant. They're at the front lines in the company's war against its employees. Employee abuse is the trench warfare of the turf battle culture of the dysfunctional company.

When things go well, the manager should always take credit and never mention the role or hard work of his or her employees. Managers should always steal any good ideas from their employees, taking them over the finish line and staking claim to them.

When things don't go well, employees should always be blamed for the manager's mistakes. Managers should always appear perfect and blame-free before their supervisors. In the eyes of the manager, it's always the employee's fault.

Managers Adrift at Sea Without Lifeboats

Another way to look at the role of managers is to think of the dysfunctional company as a rudderless ship at sea. The Cabal of Insiders is partying on the top deck. Just below them, layers of executives and upper management are in the top cabins and employees are in the steerage at the bottom of the ship.

The employees, steering the ship with oars, are following the drum beat from above by managers pounding on desks. Except, in the dysfunctional company, the drum beat is constantly changing without warning – with no plan or strategy – often at random and without a purpose. The managers are only following the confusion and noise from the cabins and deck above.

In a well-managed company, the oars would row in unison, executing a thoughtful plan reviewed and agreed upon by competent executives and management working together. The ship would move smoothly along a navigable path.

In the dysfunctional company, the result is mangled oars crashing into each other. The ship drifts aimlessly and lists. Managers are trapped in the middle, stuck in a sinking ship with no escape and no access to lifeboats above.

The one thing that keeps this happy dysfunctional family together is the one thing they all have in common: multitasking.

Multitasking, Executive Illiteracy and The Spinning Plate Theory

Multitasking is a technique used by the dysfunctional company to lower productivity. It's based on the popular management principle called **The Spinning Plate Theory of Management**, closely related to **The Juggling Balls Theory of Management**.

Multitasking is also an effective way to create smokescreens, leading to brush fires that blossom into full-blown interoffice turf wars. The right spark needed to start the next inter-silo melee could originate from two or more multitaskers screwing up simultaneously.

Multitasking is just part of the vocabulary of Company Speak for doing several things at once. Company Speak is a foreign language used by the dysfunctional company that will be discussed next in Habit Three about the importance of miscommunication. It would be too obvious to just say, "doing several things at the same time," or "doing more than one thing at a time."

The Spinning Plate Theory of Management holds that everybody at the company should be responsible for keeping as many plates as possible spinning in the air on spindles at the same time. If any plate falls, the offender will be disciplined by their supervisor. This will be followed by a note placed in their HR file, being the subject of an audit finding or getting a black mark on their annual performance review. If a plate breaks, the consequences could be even more dire.

The Juggling Balls Theory of Management is very similar, except that instead of spinning plates, people are expected to keep juggling several balls in the air at once.

Both **The Spinning Plate Theory** and **The Juggling Balls Theory** are reminiscent of a circus. In some ways, the dysfunctional company is like a circus: executives flying from trapezes and often falling, elephants crushing managers and tigers and lions eating employees.

The dysfunctional company touts multitasking as an efficient way to get more things done in less time. Instead, a lot of energy is wasted doing several tasks poorly at the same time. When multitasking, a new task starts before another is finished. An e-mail is started before the end of a meeting, and then a report is started while the e-mail is still being written. No task is ever fully completed and, in the unlikely event a task is completed, it was probably done half-assed – the e-mail during the meeting is full of typos and is contradictory, the report started during the e-mail is confusing and full of errors.

True multitaskers keep growing their personal daisy chain, until they're doing so many things at once, they lose track of what they're doing. Sticky notes with items "in process" and to-do lists with new items litter their PAWS. This is another example, again, of the key role of sticky notes in the dysfunctional company.

Some multitaskers have been known to be assigned to write hundred-page PowerPoints, combining multitasking with The Principle of the Appearance of Activity never to be viewed by anybody for phantom meetings that never occur.

Multitasking is part of the fabric of the dysfunctional company at all levels of the pyramid from the top on down to the bottom. Multitasking gets worse as one moves up the pyramid. Executives have been known to be so overwhelmed that they lose their ability to read and often have attention spans as short as a few milliseconds. This is a common phenomenon in the dysfunctional company known as Executive Illiteracy.

Anybody trying to communicate with an executive, whether their direct reports, managers, or employees, knows they have a very tight window to get their message across. An executive might blurt out in the heat of the moment, "Give me the short version," or "Tell me in twenty-five words or less." Appropriate replies might be, "We're going bankrupt," "Sales suck," "We're being sued because our product killed someone" (a bit long at eight words), or "Angry customers are burning our office down" (just right at only seven words).

Since many executives at the dysfunctional company become illiterate as they move up the pyramid, managers and employees have to use non-verbal cues to get attention. Attempting to put something in front of them with words to be read just won't work. Pictures and diagrams, even PowerPoint presentations without words but only weird shapes and symbols or funny sound effects, are the only hope of getting through.

They may flash signs with colored symbols or posters with obscene pictures in front of executives passing in the hall. They may set up an impromptu puppet show in the hallway complete with a makeshift stage and hand puppets. The puppets should depict key players in executive management – with whiny and squeaky high-pitched voices – involved in the issue at hand.

Employees and managers may dress up as clowns, jumping up and down or through burning hoops, hoping to get a few minutes of face time.

In extreme cases, employees have built bonfires of used pizza boxes in the hall.

Used pizza boxes are a handy item at the dysfunctional company. They pile up from pizza deliveries during the many all-night meetings at the office. The grease lining left on the boxes makes good kindling material. They can be stored in an empty cubicle at the office designated solely for storage of spent pizza boxes. The cubicle Row Captain should be responsible for ensuring the box supply is adequate in case of a natural disasters or a nuclear war. The vital role of Row Captains in the office will be discussed in Habit Six.

A perfect example of a turf battle caused by multitasking is a misdirected e-mail. Someone from one silo, for example, wants to send an e-mail to a silo-mate, saying "What a dumb idea," during a presentation by an executive. At the same time, the same person is writing an e-mail to ass kiss the executive, saying "What a brilliant idea!" In the heat of multitasking, since the person is simultaneously filling out an expense report, preparing for another meeting, responding to another request, taking pointless online training and shopping online or surfing porn, the two e-mails somehow get transposed. The "dumb idea" e-mail gets sent by accident to the executive, while the confused colleague gets the "brilliant idea" e-mail.

Unfortunately, not only the executive was copied on the "dumb" e-mail, but also all her direct reports and the heads of several key departments. Even before the sender of the e-mail gets drawn and quartered and then hung out to dry by HR, teams from the two silos have already put on their bicycle helmets and are duking it out in the parking lot with hockey sticks, laptops and rotten eggs from the company cafeteria.

There are two special classes of people at the dysfunctional company who are still part of the company pyramid, even though they appear to be outside the organization. They are the Lords of IT, who act like outsiders but are deeply enmeshed in every silo at every level, and road warriors, who think they're special because they're not in the office.

The Lords of IT

Everybody in the company, at all levels, from the moment they walk in the door to the day they walk out the door, whether voluntarily or not, or through death at their PAWS – needs laptops, or other computers, software and network access. This gives the Lords of IT outsize power to their numbers in the company.

Hidden behind locked doors in noisy rooms full of racks of servers, they rarely come out in public but have the power of life and death over everyone in the company. Many are nocturnal creatures who can't stand sunlight. They can grant or deny access to systems and software with the flick of a wrist, revoke or reset passwords, and repair broken equipment with their bare hands.

They also man the Helpless Desk, from where they wreak havoc on unsuspecting employees needing IT assistance.

To employees, they're invisible, only communicating from their techno rabbit hole via condescending IM messages or through angry voice mail messages. When ready to strike, they can take over an employee's computer, moving its cursor around at will, as if it was possessed by an alien creature. The employee can only take their hands off their keyboard and watch the online action unfold.

IT staff should be condescending and defensive, especially when they can't help, which sadly is often the case in the dysfunctional company. Their standard answer should be, "It's in the documentation" ("you moron" is implied). It doesn't matter that the documentation requires a PhD in computer science to understand, it's there and everyone should have read it.

IT staff should have an "us versus them" mentality. The "us" are IT, the High Priests of Technology (HPT). The "them" are the rest of the company, the Non-Technical Morons (NTM).

In the acronym-filled world of dysfunctional company jargon, IT sees itself as the HPTs against the NTMs. The importance of acronyms to dysfunctional company communication will be discussed in the next habit about poor communication. It just adds to IT being another combative team in the dysfunctional company's turf wars.

Road Warriors: Remote Part of the Pyramid

Road warriors may come from every level within the dysfunctional pyramid. Representatives from the Cabal of Insiders, for example, may meet in person with important customers to help sales reps deceive customers into thinking they're getting a good product or service. Various employees, salespeople and consultants may only be able to do their job of providing poor service in person, based on the nature of their product or service.

Road warriors may think that since they're away from the office, they aren't part of the pyramid or the petty turf battles in the office. Whether they like it or not, they're an extension of the office, and their outdoor activities are part of the indoor Olympics back home.

The after-hours stomping ground of road warriors is anywhere there is a bar: the hotel, a restaurant, or some sleazy joint whose name they can change on their expense report.

After road warriors have complained about their customers and co-workers, they can get down to real business: arguing over their travel perks.

They start by talking about which travel web sites have the best deals and how to hack the company's travel system to override expense report limits. Seasoned road warriors know how to game the dysfunctional company's travel system to avoid having to go through their cumbersome bureaucracy for approval for overpriced accommodations and airfare. Left to use the company system, they would be on flights with twenty stops and staying at the best flea-bag hotels, or even forced to pitch a tent in a public park near the customer.

Road warriors are also adept at padding expense reports, so they can conceal the porn movies they watch in their hotel room under "entertainment expenses – miscellaneous."

As they get drunker, they may start arguing about the best towels and bathrobes they permanently borrowed from hotels. Then they might get into fist fights over their airline vomit bag collections. Vomit bags are an important part of meetings at the dysfunctional company, as will be seen in Habit Four, and are a part of every employee's survival kit, as detailed in Habit Six.

But for road warriors, who are left to scavenge for their own vomit bags from airlines (again, see Habit Six for a full explanation), vomit bags are a source of bragging rights. For drunk road warriors, the pecking order of company travelers is often determined by the quality and size of their barf bag collections.

Road warriors need to remember, they aren't alone. They're still part of the dysfunctional office, even if they can't touch or see it. Drunk or not, they need to remember who, and where, they are.

The dysfunctional company may dispatch alcoholic auditors to drink uncover with road warriors. Anybody on the road should be aware some of their drinking buddies at the hotel bar may be covert company operatives. Like remote employees, road warriors are a potential source of trouble, since they're out of the watchful eye of office surveillance.

Alcoholic auditors receive extra training to learn how to conduct business under the influence. They should be lucid enough – not necessarily totally sober – while traveling to supervise road warriors for policy infractions. With the pressures auditors are already under in the office, there is no shortage of designated alcoholics in their ranks to send out for road assignments.

Other Potential Sources of Turf Battles:
Information Hoarders and Acquirees

Another subspecies – and potential source of conflict – in the dysfunctional universe is the information hoarder. These are individuals who think job security is working in secret and hiding all their work from the rest of the company. They set up bureaucratic, and sometimes even physical, checkpoints through which everyone seeking their information must pass.

Just like their counterparts, physical hoarders, they squirrel away every piece of information they have into little hutches, either in their PAWS or virtually on their laptops. Those with some IT skills may even try to commandeer their own servers to store – encrypted, of course – everything they've either currently working on or have done.

They may come from a small pool of people who do possess a unique skill required by the company. Unfortunately, the confrontational atmosphere of the dysfunctional company gives them the impression they possess secret knowledge that needs to be guarded with their life.

They mistakenly think the company can't let them go. As has been seen, nobody is safe at the dysfunctional company. What they don't realize is that they're still part of the company, not some secret society, and all their work is still on company equipment and infrastructure.

The company can still access all their work, even after they've departed. Just like every other displaced employee, information hoarders are shaken down by security before they walk out the door to make sure all their information and systems, including encryption keys, don't leave the mothership.

If the dysfunctional company has been knitted together through acquisitions, it has a mix of employees already on board from acquired companies and those hired later. If an acquired company had a different culture from its new parent, personality and bureaucratic clashes are inevitable, creating more turf battles.

When these conflicts arise, the question employees should ask are, "Were you hired or acquired?" This may not resolve the issue, but at least the confronted employees will know where they stand and can plan their counterattack appropriately.

To remote, or not to remote, that is the question

A good way to increase conflict and tension and, of course, inflame turf wars further, is to wade into the debate about whether employees should be allowed to work remotely, even if only part of the time, or must work full-time in the office.

Whether an employee works better remotely or in the office depends on the employee's work habits, the company's office culture, and the nature of their industry.

Some employees work better remotely. Others are more productive in the office. Some employees need a lot of human contact or need to be in an office environment, others don't. It all depends on the employee's personality and preferences. For some, if their remote location is their home, the "quiet" may be full of distractions and being in the office is preferred. For others, an office can be full of other types of distractions that prevent focusing on work, and they may be more productive remotely.

Meetings in certain industries may require face-to-face contact and can't be done remotely or via video conference. Some industries thrive on spontaneous hallway conversations between employees.

In the dysfunctional company, of course, this is all irrelevant. Distractions abound for both remote and office-incarcerated employees. The customary miscommunication and turf wars prevent meaningful no-strings-attached-without-politics conversations, whether in the hallway or a breakroom or remotely online.

Since the dysfunctional company treats its employees like replaceable pieces, all identical objects to be tossed around at will, it makes blanket generalizations about everyone, even when it comes to its policies on remote work. It doesn't care about individual preferences.

The dysfunctional company dictates that employees must all work in the office either full- or part-time, even if it doesn't make sense, or has nothing to do with the industry culture.

Tribalism: Another Layer of the Turf War Landscape

Beyond the pyramid, the dysfunctional company is split along tribal lines.

The tribes within the dysfunctional company can either be cross departmental boundaries or be within the same departments. They can be identified by the different clothing they wear: similar t-shirts, different colored caps, and arm bands.

They may have cool names, like the "Insane Accountants," the "Merry Marketers," or "Hell's Auditors," "Purchasing Cheapskates" and the "Facilities Fascists." IT people can't be just called "Geeks." They need a spiffy name like, "Technical Crusaders." HR could be called the "Body Snatchers."

Auditors might wear black t-shirts saying "Comply or Die" above a white skull-and-cross bones. The back of the t-shirt might say, "The gig is up. Audit is here."

When tribal members pass each in the hall, or acknowledge each other by chat for remote employees, they will flash a secret hand signal indicating their membership. This confirmation of tribal status is needed to prevent more warfare – screaming matches in the halls, flame wars online, and fist fights in meetings – than would normally occur each day.

These are just some subtle ways different tribes in the dysfunctional company communicate when they pass in the hall. They really would like to run around wearing fur pelts and antlers, and warpaint on their faces. This would be politically incorrect, since it would violate HR policies on discrimination against certain ethnic groups and could lead to an audit finding. And, nobody wants to tussle with the goons in audit.

The Atomized Company

Pyramids, silos and tribes divide up the dysfunctional company into smaller and smaller units, all competing against each other. Add in information hoarders, hired versus acquired employees, and the dysfunctional company is a pack of competing interests all vying for power. The result is an atomized company on a perpetual war footing.

The dysfunctional company may try to hide its dirty laundry from the outside world, especially its customers. But eventually the internal turmoil spills over. Its battles with customers are just a reflection of its internal battles.

The next habit will provide more detail about how silos contribute to the poor communication so vital to keeping the company dysfunctional.

Habit Three:
Poor Communication Delivers the Message

"What the hell did he say?
I didn't understand a word.
It was all acronyms and gobbledygook."

Habit Three:
Poor Communication Delivers the Message

"My psychiatrist said I had Early Onset Insanity from listening to nonsense all day."

Employees should be kept in a constant state of confusion.

Employees should be the last to know about anything, especially if it affects them directly. Today, the company says one thing, tomorrow something else, and the next day something entirely different. It's never clear what the company is really doing, or where it's going.

Employees have been known to suffer whiplash from wildly jerking their head back and forth whenever they hear news announcements. It's not unusual to see large numbers of employees at the dysfunctional company walking around like zombies with neck braces. Zombies walking around the office, with or without neck braces, are another sign of a dysfunctional company.

In addition to neck braces, some employees may have their heads wrapped in bandages from banging their heads on the wall. Others may have bandages on their wrists from attempting to slash themselves.

The effective use of poor communication is essential to the functioning of the dysfunctional company. Missives come not only from the Cabal of Insiders on high. They also come from a multitude of departments. They're constantly spewing out bulletins and notices for this or that pointless new program or useless activity.

This habit deals with internal communication with employees. Poor external communication to customers through deceptive and confusing marketing is covered in detail in Habit Five about customer relations.

Effective poor communication is background noise and static. It makes employees heads spin to the point where they can't think straight. They may not even know any more what business the company is in. It's not clear from its messaging if the company knows either what business it's in. This is the dysfunctional company. It's not in the business of doing business. It's in the business of producing spin, as reflected in its cockeyed communication. It's in the business of bureaucracy building and office politics, definitely not producing products or services and definitely not sales or customer service.

There can never be too much communication in the dysfunctional company. Employees need to be constantly misinformed about what the company is really doing. Communication can be constipated, being forced onto employees in dribs and drabs, or like diarrhea, loose and flowing non-stop. Constipated communication keeps employees wondering. Diarrhea overwhelms them to the point of confusion. In the dysfunctional company, diarrhea communication is preferred.

Another effective way to complicate things is through obfuscated communication planted around the office. Dysfunctional companies have propaganda machines that would make Stalin jealous. They have banners and posters with empty company slogans, as seen in Habit One, strung around the office and even screen savers on their laptops, where employees, already harassed by excessive announcements by e-mail, can't avoid them.

The Silo: Ideal Structure for Poor Communication

As was seen in Habit Two, the silo is the ideal form of organization for the dysfunctional company, particularly for keeping miscommunication high between siloed departments. Miscommunication helps keep tensions high between departments and among staff within departments. And stress and tension are what the dysfunctional company is all about.

Nobody should be given a moment of peace. Nobody should have time to think about the deluge of information thrown at them.

In the absence of credible sources of information, employees revert to informal communication networks. These are underground networks along tribal lines, as was seen in Habit Two, and through special office spaces, breakrooms and bathrooms, discussed in this Habit. There's nothing like tribalism and breakrooms and bathrooms for spreading misinformation throughout the dysfunctional company.

Often overlooked is forced socializing, another good way to pass incorrect information through the ranks, especially if it involves alcohol. That will guarantee lips will loosen up, and God knows what somebody will say. As will be discussed in Habit Six, employees have to attend mandatory social events, particularly if it gets in the way of work. A social event, forced or not, is always better than working, or non-working, as may be the case in the dysfunctional company. The mostly mundane tasks at the dysfunctional company are best done, anyways, in an inebriated state.

Both real and fake news spreads through these underground railroads faster than through "official" channels.

Breakrooms and Bathrooms: Critical Communication Channels

Breakrooms and bathrooms serve as vital communication links in the dysfunctional company, since above ground communication from the company can't be trusted. Breakrooms and bathrooms are where the vast informal underground communication network at the dysfunctional company operates.

Breakrooms are small areas in the office stocked with refreshments and snacks, where employees can mingle. Most employees need something stiffer than a soft drink and a bag of potato chips to get through the day. But the breakroom isn't really about midday pick-me-ups. It's about getting the latest scoop on what's really going on at the office.

The breakroom is the modern equivalent of the famous "water cooler," where employees used to gather to pass on secret information. Today, what used to be the water cooler is a breakroom stocked with hi-tech coffee makers, a refrigerator with soft drinks and vending machines. They may even have a sink and silverware for employees who bring their meals to work to avoid food poisoning in the company cafeteria.

This is a rare moment for employees to leave their PAWS, spread their legs for a few minutes and spread gossip and rumors about their coworkers. They can also pass along other misinformation they may have picked up during the day from other unreliable random sources around the office. With only lies and bullshit being shoved down their throats the rest of the day, employees can only guess who is doing what in the office. The breakroom is where employees try to untangle – and "process," if you will – the daily verbal garbage.

Remote employees have their own online breakrooms. They can set up private chat rooms, restricted to members of their various cliques, to meet virtually and go through the same rituals as their office counterparts to sort out the day's nonsense. They can also bring their own refreshments and, if carefully concealed in innocuous containers, alcoholic beverages.

Camouflage, of course, is needed to distract the spies in audit and security, observing them through surveillance software planted on their laptops. Though drinking on the job is forbidden, even in the dysfunctional company, it's often necessary to deal with office craziness.

Bathrooms are the other vital information communications conduit in the dysfunctional company. Here, employees and management at different levels, who don't normally mix, can rub elbows. When nature calls, even in the dysfunctional company, everybody must answer the door. Everybody must go there at some point in the day. Ultimately, some business will always end up in the bathroom. This is known as the **Bathroom Communication Rule**.

The one exception is the Cabal of Insiders, who has its own bathroom with gold-plated sinks and toilet seats to not have to condescend to take a crap near their workers. Their bathrooms are far from employees and are inaccessible anyways without special key cards. The isolation of their bathrooms is another way they shield their secret rituals from the rest of the company.

Outside the Cabal, there is no better way for employees and management to bond than to be taking a whiz or dump in neighboring stalls in the bathroom. They can chit chat about sports or fashions or the latest news of the world to break the ice and then talk about real business.

The golf course may be the exclusive preserve of executives and management, but the bathroom belongs to everyone. Whoever said real business takes place on the golf course doesn't understand the dysfunctional company. The real business gets done in the bathroom.

The prepared employee will always bring an envelope or manila file with their open items to the bathroom. These can conveniently fall on the floor or be discreetly slipped under the stall door or divider of the neighboring stall where the executive or manager is temporarily located. Open items might include the proposal that seems to be perpetually ignored, or maybe the expense report for sticky notes that has been sitting unpaid for months.

Aggressive employees have been known to hang around with their manila folders outside bathroom doors. When they spot an executive going in the bathroom, they rush in, papers in hand, ready to shove them in the waiting executive's stall. As every astute employee knows, an executive on the can is a captive executive.

Of course, male employees will need a female accomplice if the bathroom bound executive is female, and vice versa for female employees trying to get the attention of a male executive answering the call of nature.

The more constipated the manager, the more likely they're trapped on the ceramic throne and in need of something to help push things out. The more constipated, the longer their attention span. Items casually slipped under their nose in the stall might be just the trick to get more than their bowels moving. Loose office papers in bathroom stalls are known as the laxative of bureaucracy.

Employees need to time their bathroom breaks carefully. They need to be spaced out to not trigger a negative comment in their annual performance review.

Every bathroom break is logged whenever an employee enters the door. Each break is added to the employee's **Bathroom Attendance Ratio (BAR)**, which is the number of times the employee goes to the bathroom each day. The BAR can also be converted to time spent in the bathroom and then expressed as a percentage of an eight-hour day, for example.

If all else fails, the patient employee, spotting their target executive entering the bathroom, can just hang around outside the door and pounce when the target has left after completing nature's duties. This is a clever workaround to effectively achieve the same bathroom results while keeping the BAR low.

As will be seen in Habit Six about employee annual reviews, the BAR is just another metric used to transform the employee from a human into a number. It contributes to the impersonal atmosphere of the dysfunctional company. Good employees are expected to keep their BAR down as low as possible.

Employees also need to be aware they are still under constant surveillance by audit and security, even in breakrooms and bathrooms. Breakrooms should have security cameras to watch employees. Bathrooms may not have cameras, but they're probably still bugged with sensitive listening devices, to filter out the sounds of nature. The company secret police are making sure employees are only going to bathrooms to do the work of nature and not the work of overthrowing the company.

All Communication Must Be Vertical

As part of the turf battles discussed in Habit Two, all communication in the dysfunctional company must be vertical, meaning within silos. Horizontal communication can lead to cooperation between departments – another danger to dysfunctional behavior.

Direct communication between employees, even in the same department, should be strongly discouraged. This is known as the **Vertical**

Communication Only Policy, part of the company communication policy and vigorously enforced by auditors.

Other than greetings in the morning, even employees sitting next to each or in neighboring cubicles shouldn't be allowed to talk to each other, especially about what might be mistaken for productive company business. If they need to communicate, one employee should send an e-mail to his or her supervisor, who in turn forwards it up to his or her supervisor and on up the chain, even up to the CEO, if necessary. Like a bullet shot straight up in the air, the message should come back down from above through the second employee's parallel silo and hit him or her in the head.

If the second employee needs to respond, the answer should go back up through the same chain of command back from where it first started. This seesaw should bounce back and forth as long as necessary until the question is resolved, which, in the dysfunctional company, may be never. In this way, turfs and silos are driven down from the department level, cleaving the company down further to the smallest company unit, the employee.

As a side note, morning greetings, as well, should be severely restricted since they may actually create a congenial work environment and a mistaken sense of employee community – not encouraged in the dysfunctional company. These are another threat to the dysfunctional company. A hostile and combative work environment with employees on the defensive is a healthy dysfunctional one.

A Typical Miscommunication Event

A maintenance guy overhears two executives talking in adjacent urinals about plans to close a department and layoff its staff. The maintenance guy goes and tells his friend in accounting that massive layoffs are coming. The person in accounting tells someone in IT, who is fixing her laptop, and he tells his buddy in facilities management. She then tells her friend in marketing, who tells his friend in HR that he heard there will be massive layoffs and half the company will be outsourced overseas. And so on, until it ricochets throughout the company faster than a speeding bullet.

To spice things up, someone may throw in a comment about Martians landing in the parking lot and taking over the company. This probably came from another rumor circulating simultaneously from another bathroom conversation in another part of the building about a possible merger. The

"Martians" is a coded reference to the barbarians from another company who might be planning to sack Rome.

The underground network is an improvement over the way news normally travels at glacial speed through aboveboard channels. By the time it reaches the last person in the chain, say, the security guard at the front door, everybody in the company thinks they're about to lose their job and that the company is going out of business and shutting down, or maybe being swallowed up by creatures from outer space.

By now, everybody in the company is in a state of panic and confusion, more so than the baseline level of hysteria on a normal day.

The groundwork for informal communication now laid, either through tribal networks, or breakrooms and bathrooms, or forced socializing, it's time to turn to official communication – the Business Blocker Twins (BBT). BBT consists of e-mail, followed by meetings.

The Importance of Excessive E-mail

The first line in the disinformation war against employees in the BBT duet is e-mail. There are two types of e-mail spam in the dysfunctional company.

The first is e-mail that comes from on high, such as the Cabal of Insiders or other department heads, and the other is internal e-mail between employees.

Technology is a double-edged sword in the dysfunctional company. It can be used for, or against, employees and customers. It can ease work flow, not something the dysfunctional is good at, or it can be a weapon against employees or customers to hound and harass them into submission.

E-mail is an example of a technology in the dysfunctional company's arsenal of destructive weapons.

Whether from on high, or from sideways, employees should be receiving a constant stream of e-mails throughout the day, distracting them until they can't concentrate. It ranges from the pointless announcements from executives or management to e-mails from co-workers about work, or what is passing as work, again, The Principle of the Appearance of Activity.

The nonsense from above, and other company pronouncements, can be ditched in the trash bin immediately, as soon as it reaches the inbox. The tech-savvy employee will know how to set up a filter to dispose of these e-mails when they arrive.

Setting up e-mail filters for company announcements is just another time-wasting survival mechanism for the employee.

E-mails can be divided further into "**Love Notes**" and "**Nasty Grams.**" The Love Notes are when things are going well, which is rare in the dysfunctional company. The "Nasty Grams" are from other employees when there are problems, which is the norm, or from pissed off customers, also the norm.

Nasty Grams may also be system-generated messages threatening the employee. Examples are a warning that a time sheet needs to be filed, and that punishment may include anything from a slap on the face in public up to dismissal. The sane employee might choose dismissal.

Another Nasty Gram might be a rejection of a multi-page online application for office supplies, saying the box for the employee's blood type wasn't filled out. The helpless employee can't respond. There is no return e-mail to an anonymous system bot.

Somewhere in between the Love Note and the Nasty Gram are other system-generated messages, reminding the employee of some upcoming forced social activity, or a required training that has nothing to do with the employee's job function.

It's important for employees to receive the correct training for their job role, which the dysfunctional company may, or may not, provide. There are those pesky ethics and HR trainings that pop up right in the middle of the day, when the employee is in the middle of an important project. Nothing is too annoying at the dysfunctional company. Anything to pester employees and to block real work is fair game.

Every E-mail Must Always Be Answered

E-mail can never be ignored. It should keep flooding in throughout the day, maybe even every second. It should be a bottomless pit of quicksand with no escape where sunlight isn't visible. It should fill up the employee's inbox until it freezes their e-mail system. The employee will be forced to call the Helpless Desk in IT to archive or clear out their e-mail. Another adventure into the heart of bureaucratic darkness begins.

E-mails between employees are known as **Horizontal Communication Disturbances (HCD)**, since they're usually moving between employees at similar levels in the hierarchy. Occasionally, an e-mail will go vertical, in this case called a **Vertical Communication Disturbance (VCD)**, either when the e-mail is unanswered, or if it starts from above, in the case of an executive or someone in the Cabal of Insiders.

Unanswered e-mails, of course, need to be escalated, turning them into VCDs. If there isn't an answer after one day, then the e-mail should be sent again with the employee's supervisor copied. If the e-mail still isn't answered a second day, then it should be sent again to the supervisor's supervisor and everybody else previously copied. This process of adding successive layers in the bureaucratic chain of command should continue every day until the e-mail is answered. If it remains unanswered until it reaches the highest levels of management, or beyond, into executive outer space, someone in the stratosphere will eventually need to start screaming to get a reply.

In the case of an e-mail originating from executive hyperspace, the e-mail disturbance flows down, another example of a VCD. Executive directives by e-mail are usually forwarded down the bureaucracy immediately.

In this VCD scenario, an executive sends a missive to his or her direct report, say, a vice president, who, in turn, simply forwards it to his or her underling director, who then moves it on to the next manager in the feeding chain, and then on down to the employee. The e-mail rolls downhill and snowballs into a masterpiece of poor and confused messaging as it grows and picks up layers of bullshit along the way.

The dysfunctional company makes sure everybody gets more e-mails than can be answered in a lifetime, guaranteeing some will be orphaned and never answered. Excessive e-mail may even be company policy, added to the jungle of rules audit and HR may use against the employee. Not having enough e-mails is never a positive in the employee's annual performance review.

Since everybody at all levels at the dysfunctional company is always trying to pass the buck, anyways, they end up forwarding e-mails here and there at random, maybe to complete strangers, just to lighten the load.

Some employees may have nervous breakdowns from looking at their overflowing inbox at inopportune moments during the day, such as during a mandatory meeting, and run into the hall and start screaming. Some have even been known to throw their laptops up in the air or smash them against a wall. This, or course, doesn't solve the problem. IT just replaces their laptop, often the same day, and the e-mail is still there, waiting patiently for action or, as usually happens at the dysfunctional company, inaction.

After the employee has been heavily sedated and propped up at their PAWS, they will see their shiny new laptop waiting for them. Before they can turn it on, of course, they will have to provide the required dozens of signatures to confirm they received their new equipment.

Remote employees who have e-mail-induced nervous breakdowns may cut-and-paste snippets of e-mails, particularly if they're confidential or controversial, in chat rooms and company message boards, adding profanity, signaling they've gone off the rails and need psychotherapy or medication.

A Typical E-mail Chain Letter

Constant e-mails from other employees around the company all day long are the most annoying and damaging. With so many walls and barriers between and within departments, employees are starved for the information they need for their job. They become information prowlers. E-mail is the best way to scrounge around to get any tidbits needed for work.

It starts with a simple e-mail. It could be a request for information. It could be a request for an approval. It could be granting an approval. It could be providing information. It could be responding to a customer. It could be total bullshit, or maybe just the latest sports pool.

Yet, from one small e-mall, like weeds overtaking a lawn, a fresh bureaucratic disaster grows. Meetings – especially regular repetitive meetings – are always the preferred business blocker. A tiny e-mail is all it takes to start the process to engage the bureaucratic machinery to start a meeting. All it takes is one small step – the click of a mouse – and Meeting Hell awaits.

The employee sends an innocent e-mail about a project for a customer to her supervisor. Suddenly, she realizes she should have copied legal. There isn't any outstanding legal issue – yet – but the dysfunctional company is always getting sued. It's best to be proactive and copy them at the beginning of the e-mail chain.

She starts thinking, always dangerous at the dysfunctional company since it might cause a fire, and figures out the project will require extra hours. She copies project management to request more hours on her time sheet. The project is already behind schedule even before it started because some anonymous idiot in the bureaucracy needed more useless information – the height and weight of everybody on the project team – as part of more unnecessary paperwork.

Someone is going to get offended by some inappropriate comment at some point. It's better to copy HR early on just to be safe. There will probably be an impact on IT resources – better to copy them too. There will probably be a cost overrun, especially since the project will be understaffed or poorly staffed or just poorly handled – better notify accounting. Marketing will want to know when the project starts. They should be added.

Executive sponsors and managers, especially if they're not directly involved in the day-to-day work of the project, will want hourly, if not minute-by-minute updates with every gory detail. Facilities will need to be copied, since conference rooms will need to be scheduled. Purchasing will need to be notified so additional sticky notes can be ordered for project progress reports.

Meetings will need to be scheduled. Committees will need to be set up. Reports will need to be generated. Maybe a whole new parallel bureaucracy will need to be created to handle the anticipated extra work load.

Audit and security will need to be copied, because the little spies just have to know everything going on. The cafeteria may be called on to provide something edible to participants trapped in long meetings in sealed conference rooms with no ventilation. It's a good idea to copy them too.

Security guards at the entrance to the office should be notified, since more ambulances will be coming to ferry away injured or dead employees, mostly from self-inflicted wounds, who were trying to get the project done.

Finally, sanitation will need to be on the e-mail, since bathrooms may be overcrowded when everybody is let out at the same time for bio breaks.

By now, everybody in the company has been copied on a massive e-mail chain. What started as a simple e-mail is now a chain letter snaking its way through the entire company.

The entire company has been paralyzed by a single e-mail. Just another e-mail-induced work stoppage. Just another day in the office at the dysfunctional company.

Another closely-related, yet still brilliant, e-mail tactic for causing company paralysis is the **Dump and Run** (the infamous **D&R**). This is where an employee sends an e-mail about a controversial subject and forgets about it. This is also known as the Ignored Sent E-mail, or the Abandoned E-mail. Whatever the e-mail says, it will be long and involved and ruffle a lot of feathers around the company. In the D&R, the employee sends the e-mail just before leaving for the day and then shuts down their laptop and ignores the flood of mostly angry and hostile responses.

Another official channel for spreading company trash talk is the infamous Town Hall.

The Town Hall:
Propaganda and Disinformation Events

The so-called **Town Hall** is another way the dysfunctional company transmits misinformation to employees. The Town Hall is where someone from the Cabal of Insiders descends from their ivory tower to appear in person in front of employees.

Town Halls could be for just a particular department or group of employees, or for the entire company, depending on the size and importance of the misguided message the company is delivering.

The member of the Cabal and his or her lieutenants are flanked on either side of the podium by a small army of administrative and support staff. They look like body guards protecting a head of state. This gives the anointed executive a mythical aura of being a superhuman leader, descended from heaven, or maybe just from the Gods of Business.

Employees can attend in person, or virtually, by dialing in or by video conference or Zoom. Employees may even be given a rare exemption from attending other meetings (normally required under Habit Four) to honor the visiting company dignitary.

The entrances to the Town Hall should be protected by security personnel to prevent employees from escaping. Remote employees already have software on their laptop locking them into the event. Attempts at trying to logout of the Town Hall or do other activity, especially if work-related, will be logged and sent to audit for review.

Security personnel onsite also prevent employees from rushing the podium to get selfies with their leader. Employees crave selfies with members of the Cabal in the mistaken belief they are making a connection with a center of power who can help them during a crisis. They think they are networking with the right people in the company. Sadly, such enthusiastic employees are often at the top of the death list to be let go during a mass layoff.

The Town Hall is supposed to be a question-and-answer session, where employees can freely ask executives questions directly. This is just an illusion. Everything presented should be staged and artificial to put the company in the best possible light. Nothing should be ad-lib or impromptu. Nothing additional should be added during the presentation.

The Town Hall should be rehearsed like a theatrical production. But then, it is a theatrical production. It's the theater of the absurd called the dysfunctional company.

If the company is in trouble, which is where the dysfunctional company is usually heading, if not there already, the presentation will be like a pep talk on the deck of the Titanic. Executives should be as out-of-touch as much as possible from the reality of the company and its employees.

The timing of Town Halls is critical. It's best to hold a Town Hall just before a massive layoff or another redundant and pointless reorganization. The executive can portray the company through rose-colored glasses, saying everything is just fine, sales are strong, the company is growing. This is perfect for giving employees a false sense of security and then loosening them up before the big kill.

If an employee asks a difficult question, he or she should be approached from both sides by two security personnel, who each pick up the employee by an arm, and lift him or her from their seat. The offending employee is then dragged through the building to the entrance and dumped in the parking lot.

The offending employee shouldn't be let back into the building until the end of the Town Hall. This gives the employee time to think about their inappropriate behavior. They will learn to never again ask a question of anyone in the Cabal.

For a remote employee who asks a difficult question, their laptop screen will go blank and they will be locked out of the Town Hall. A message will appear on their screen, saying, "You have been expelled from the Town Hall for asking an unapproved question. Your access will be restored at the conclusion of the event. We thank you for your understanding."

The brutal suppression of honest questions will scare other participants at the Town Hall into keeping quiet. This will allow the presenter to continue spewing the rest of their pre-planned bullshit without interference.

At the end of the Town Hall, the executive is escorted out of the room by his or her assistants and disappears into the night. The employees return to whatever they were doing and continue the rest of their unproductive day.

Besides Town Halls, the dysfunctional company may also have other surprise propaganda events. These always happen when least expected and when the employee is in the middle of something. They start with a sudden announcement, for both office and remote employees, that they're required to attend a presentation.

Employees in the office will be marched in formation from their PAWS and then locked in a conference room. Remote employees will notice their laptops have been taken over by strange bureaucratic creatures and will be locked into the presentation. They will be blocked from whatever work, or non-work, they were doing.

After the lights are dimmed, a video starts showing happy employees, probably tranquilized and forced to say some canned garbage about how great the company is. They may even talk about how their "contributions" to the company "made a difference." None of this makes sense, of course, since it's impossible for employees to make a difference at the dysfunctional company. They're ignored and tossed out the door, as will be seen in Habit Six about driving out good employees.

Employees who have spoken up, or just been found guilty of an audit finding, may have already gone through the same propaganda events in that other conduit of misinformation: company training.

Company Training:
Correction Camps and Indoctrination

When used effectively, **Company Training** is another tool for keeping employees throughout the dysfunctional company disinformed. Companies can provide useful and necessary training about the product or service, or unrelated training, for example, about basic business skills. The dysfunctional company, on the other hand, has tons of additional training employees must endure, mostly worthless and unrelated to the employee's job.

Training is also a cover for the dysfunctional company's correction camps for straightening out employees violating policies and procedures or trying to think independently.

Training can be presented remotely through the employee's laptop, or live to a group in a conference room or offsite at either another company facility or an outside location, such as a hotel or meeting center. Offsite training can be combined with forced socializing to prolong the pain.

As with everything else in the dysfunctional company, training is haphazard. It doesn't matter if it's on-demand or live, local or offsite, it should still be scheduled at random and in a way that is the most inconvenient for the employee. Employees should have no idea when the training rabbit will unexpectedly pop out of the hat with a message, usually by e-mail, saying the employee must attend such-and-such mandatory training or face severe punishment, usually a public lashing in the company cafeteria before a crowd of curious spectators.

As with all the other random communication in the dysfunctional company, employees shouldn't be able to plan their work around mandatory trainings. Advance planning would make sense and is, therefore, unacceptable. E-mails announcing a required training course should come from an anonymous e-mail address that can't accept replies and that doesn't have any contact person for asking questions. The training should be automatically added to the employee's calendar and can't be removed or rescheduled.

Training can be either voluntary or required. Voluntary training might include helpful courses about implementation of the product or service or new features and updates. It might be about how to use and repair the product, or how to improve the service. It could also include soft skills like manager training, or time and people management.

In the dysfunctional company, these are simply feel-good courses offered to pacify employees. They portray ideal workplaces where people get along and actually listen and respect each other. Nothing like the dysfunctional company. There is no office politics or ego-driven power games. There are no unnecessary rules and crippling procedures. There is no suffocating bureaucracy. Everything gets done. Everything is smooth. Customers get service and are happy.

None of what employees learn in training can be put into practice at the dysfunctional company, anyways. Once they finish training, they go back into the company's dark alleys, where they face reality. Since the pie-in-the-sky world shown in training isn't anything like the dysfunctional company, training ends up being a waste of time.

Some training may be required by local laws or industry regulations. Training could be about labor laws, sexual harassment, spotting fraud and money laundering, cybersecurity and online safety, or reporting ethics violations. While such training may be noble, and even practical or useful, the dysfunctional company makes it as inconvenient as possible to do the training. It schedules training at the last minute, forcing the employee to cram it into their already packed schedule, then threatens the employee – with excessive e-mails, of course – if training isn't completed on time.

Legally or regulatory mandated training is often provided online or via computer-based software. These packages are usually professionally done slick and neat packages from third-party training outfits. They couldn't have been produced by the dysfunctional company, which can barely get its own products and services out the door, let alone produce something additional for internal use. They would be caught up in the dysfunctional company's customary bureaucratic and scheduling nightmares and never get done.

Other training the dysfunctional company may mandate is for so-called soft skills. This means groups of employees standing in circles holding hands and chanting the latest psychobabble hymns. Other useless activities might include one group of participants deliberately falling, while another group tries to catch them before they hit the floor. This supposedly establishes bonds of trust between employees.

Since employees rarely trust each other in the dysfunctional company, nobody stops their fellow employees from falling down, and they get injured when they hit the floor. Like honesty and openness, trust is a rare commodity at the dysfunctional company.

Yet other "soft" training might include wearing colored badges and trying to identify each other's personality flaws. This helps employees identify who they can pick on and abuse in the office after training.

Employees arrested by audit are in for a special treat. Their training takes place at specially designed company correction camps. If the company has resources, it should have a dedicated training facility. If not, they may have to share existing rooms and facilities used for other training. It's not a good idea to mix employees in normal training with those attending correction training. Employees are already tortured enough just working for the dysfunctional company, and seeing the real torture in correction training isn't good for morale.

The training facility should be a secluded building, far from the company's offices, in a wooded area surrounded by animals and birds. A flamingo standing on one leg next to a running brook is a nice touch. The chirping birds and pastoral setting calms the nerves of attendees for the brutal indoctrination yet to come. There shouldn't be any predatory animals, like lions or bears preying on other wildlife, since this would be too much like the office and might disturb the ambiance for training attendees.

The facility should have guest rooms and a dining area, where meals are served, just like a hotel. The bathrooms should have single stalls, allowing only one employee at a time, to prevent the bathroom fraternizing normally going on in the office. The idea is to keep attendees as isolated – trapped might be too strong a word – at the facility.

During training, employees are strapped into their seats and forced to watch non-stop propaganda films about the company for hours. The films show employees happily working at the company. To add to the effect, they may also show young employees fresh out of school, taking about the great things they will do at the company and the great future they have ahead of them.

At some sessions, the lights are dimmed and attendees must stand up, put their hand over their heart and chant slogans about how lucky they are to be working for the greatest dysfunctional company in history. They may also chant phony positive affirmations about how the company always wins, failure never happens, their product or service is the best, or the sky is always blue and it never rains.

This all adds to the psychological indoctrination required to stay sane at the dysfunctional company.

During bio and smoking breaks, training inmates can go into the courtyard and stand in a circle and exchange cigarettes and war stories:

Someone will open with, "What are you in for?"

"I tried to expense my sticky notes (see Habit One)."
"I tried to help a customer" (see Habit Five).
"I didn't have enough company swag on my desk" (see Habit Six).
"I tried to submit a proposal about a good idea I had (see Habit One)."
"I violated the Clean Desk Policy" (see Habit Five).
"I missed a meeting (see Habit Four)."

Then, there are the confused employees, who have no idea why they're in after school detention: "I don't know what policy I violated. I don't know what I did. I was just picked up in the hall by hostile auditors."

And then the most egregious of company violations: "I was trying to get work done."

Even more serious, considered a capital offense: "I skipped a forced socializing event because I had work to do."

After finishing their sentence at the company correction camp, employees are thrown back into the general prison population at the dysfunctional company. The experience should be so traumatic and painful, the offending employee learns to never violate a company policy again.

Company Dialects Should be Mutually Unintelligible

Each department within the company should have its own lingo, like a language with different dialects. The heavy use of jargon and technical terms only understood by narrow groups within the company should be encouraged. This contributes to the tribal nature of the dysfunctional company, where employee relations, and relations between management and employees, is always seen as "us versus them."

Insider lingo should be used extensively in meetings. It should make meetings incomprehensible. This leads to misunderstandings and conflict between employees. Employees won't know what each other are saying.

IT staff have their own underground slang not understood by non-technical people, particularly business types. A "cloud" isn't something in the sky. It's the "allocation of resources." It can't be just explained as providing computer services over the Internet, such as servers, databases, networks or storage. That would be too easy, and simple communication is not encouraged at the dysfunctional company. It might not be obvious, if not explained properly, that a "server" doesn't bring food. It's another type of computer shared by several users. The secret language of IT is formidable.

If communication appears to be clearing up, and there might be a meeting of the minds, the communication must be stopped immediately. The offending employees should be reprimanded for making something understandable. An audit finding will follow for violating company policy against understandable communication.

Company Speak Should Replace Human Language

Company Speak is essential to keeping employees uninformed, confused and off base, all necessary for keeping the company dysfunctional. And, of course, Company Speak should be complicated and convoluted. Getting directly to the point is not allowed. In the spirit of Habit One, if it makes sense, or simple, it just shouldn't be said.

There are thousands of mutually unintelligible dialects of Company Speak. Not only does it create barriers between companies, particularly dysfunctional ones, it creates barriers within organizations. The dysfunctional company is like a mountainous country with villages separated by deep valleys.

In this proverbial mountain kingdom, even though the villagers speak the same language, since they're physically cut off from each other, their dialects are mutually unintelligible. In the dysfunctional company, cubical dwellers are isolated in rows, making physical communication difficult. With Company Speak thrown in, crisp and clear communication becomes impossible.

The inability to communicate is vital to keeping the company divided and dysfunctional. It doesn't matter whether the two cubical villagers are in adjoining rows or on opposite sides of the world, speaking fluent Company Speak, they still won't have any idea what each other is saying.

To add to the fun, desk phones should be removed from all PAWSs. This forces everybody to only use e-mail, chat, internal office IM, or their cell phone or tin cans with strings to communicate. Direct human contact between employees, other than in e-mail or meetings, of course, should be avoided as much as possible.

Desk phones should be removed from any PAWS, since they're obsolete. Desk phones are only seen, in any case, in technology-challenged dysfunctional companies, who might also still be using air tubes to move documents around the office.

Bullhorns are another way for employees to communicate, especially for communication across several rows of cubicles. This is much better than just yelling "Hey, You. I need my expense report approved," or "Yo, bro, I need a stapler," which might not be heard above the normal din in the office.

Employees should be prepared to bring their own bullhorns, since purchasing rarely has enough in stock when needed. Even if they do, they're probably broken or outdated.

No matter what medium is used for transmitting Company Speak, it must replace all human language at the dysfunctional company.

Little Downsides Need to Be Covered

Users of Company Speak talk about "paradigm shifts," "continuums," "skill sets," and "cost effectiveness." Projects have been "actualized" or "rationalized" with "little downside." In some places, little downsides should be covered with longer skirts or pants. But in the dysfunctional company, endless debates take place about little downsides without HR even flinching.

Not only is this gobbledygook nonsense within the dysfunctional company, it's confusing to civilians – particularly outsiders who don't know the company's secret rituals and gang colors.

If a dysfunctional company employee asked a civilian on the street outside the office about a paradigm shift, they would probably get a dazed look. The alert civilian would suddenly realize they were talking to an escaped inmate from the nearby dysfunctional company. They would then point to a service station down the street where the employee could have their shock absorbers replaced to realign their paradigm.

Dysfunctional companies "rationalize," "right-size," "downsize," "restructure," and "lay off." They may also use this little gem: "Reduction in Force," affectionately known as a RIF. What ever happened to just plain, "You're fired"? But no, that would be too easy and too obvious. It can't be used by the dysfunctional company.

Another beauty is the Performance Improvement Program, affectionately called a PIP. This is the last step in the paper trail for employees about to be canned. Just calling it simply "probation" would violate this Habit.

PIPs will be discussed in more detail, as they relate to employee termination – or more accurately execution and liquidation – in Habit Six.

Company Speak plays a key role in how the dysfunctional company brainwash its employees. Mistakenly called orientation, new employees are strapped to chairs in dark rooms and forced to watch videos for hours on end with speeches by company executives, some of whom died or went insane long ago. If this fails to produce the desired result – an employee who can regurgitate company slogans by heart – they get barcoded as will be explained in Habit Six.

Habit Six goes into more detail about exactly what is involved in **Employee Disorientation** training.

Here's a snippet of Company Speak to get a feel for its complexity and some of its nuances:

There are insufficient resources allocated in the plan for this fiscal year to allow appropriate FTE count to be executed for the proposed project to be effective under the current five-year strategy goal of maximizing growth and planning.

The subtitle to this foreign language film should read:

We don't have enough money in the budget this year to hire the people we need to complete the project on time.

In the untranslated piece, one acronym (FTE or Full-Time Equivalent, fluent gibberish meaning "full-time employee") was thrown in. Acronyms are essential to muddying Company Speak further and making it more cryptic. Acronyms should be used as much as possible. The goal of the dysfunctional company is to eventually replace all words with acronyms. If it can't be baked into an acronym, it shouldn't be said.

The Power of Acronyms

The dysfunctional company believes acronyms streamline processes by shortening language. Acronyms are actually the ultimate secret weapon for creating confused communication.

If all else fails, acronyms are the nuclear weapon of choice. In addition, acronyms shouldn't be the same throughout the dysfunctional company. Different divisions, even different rows of cubicles and workspaces within one office, should use different acronyms.

Even though they're outside the office, remote employees participate in acronym games through their chat rooms and messaging applications. They might even have their own acronyms used only by their virtual brethren in addition to those used by their brick-and-mortar counterparts. Whether in the office or remote, the lack of consistent language fragments the dysfunctional company further into smaller and smaller competing units.

Since no real work is getting done at the company anyways, a fun idea that wastes time is to have a contest among employees to create a sentence consisting entirely of acronyms with as few nouns and verbs as possible.

Points will be deducted for any nouns or verbs remaining in the sentence. Contestants can only use acronyms currently used by the dysfunctional company. The creation of new acronyms during a match disqualifies the employee and will be reported to HR for disciplinary action and a black mark on their file.

Employees who consistently win acronym contests can get nominated to an Acronym Committee whose sole responsibility is to create new acronyms. The lucky winners are probably employees who are unable to communicate with other employees in full sentences, instead speaking in grunts, strange noises and hand gestures, high-pitched whistles and whose internal IM messages consist only of emoticons.

Committee members salivate at the chance to be real bureaucrats. They can send tons of e-mails to each other throughout the day with acronym suggestions and can hold regular meetings to create more bottlenecks. They are the only employees anointed with the honor of being able to create acronyms. They help build the dysfunctional company's acronym vocabulary and are responsible for putting together acronym dictionaries. Other less talented employees aren't allowed to create acronyms under punishment by a letter in their personnel file.

Acronym creation is another example of **Unproductive Bureaucratic Activity (UBA**, pronounced OO-buh), ideal for the dysfunctional company. The importance of UBA hours on employee time sheets will be covered in Habit Six about employee performance reviews.

In the spirit of Dysfunctional Company Acronym Creation (DCAC), pronunciation instructions must accompany any freshly minted acronym. These instructions should also include which syllable is to be stressed. Of course, this may vary between different regions of the company. In this example, DCAC is pronounced "DEE-kak" with the stress on the DEE, capitalized here for emphasis.

Employees with extra hours of UBAs in their time sheets from DCAC are eligible to win prizes, including an all-expense paid trip to the company retreat in Antarctica – a real incentive to the closet acronym creators in the office.

Translated Examples of Company Speak

The following are a couple of examples of Company Speak, showing how fundamental it is to the functioning of the dysfunctional company:

Here's a real winner:

> *We're reducing the number of associates at our domestic facilities due to a realignment of our business process.*

The envelope please (imagine tearing) for the translation:

We're firing half our staff because we're screwed up, we don't know what we're doing, and this should, at least, save us money.

Does that realignment include a lube job and a filter change, or will the radiator have to be flushed too?

The following are a sampling of other choice words from the dysfunctional company vocabulary with their definitions:

- Challenging Role – "You suck and have been demoted."

- Re-engineering – Procedures to get groups of employees or departments fired.

- Empowerment – "You can say what you want but you're still a peon, and ultimately you'll have to shut up and do as you're told."

- Bandwidth – A way for employees to communicate across departments by radio signals.

- Associates and Guests – Euphemisms for "employee" and "customers" respectively.

- Mental Map – Used to get out of the building in case of a fire.

A complete glossary of Company Speak would fill a dictionary. But most dysfunctional companies are so screwed up, they couldn't even get a dictionary together without endless committees, meetings, studies, approvals and paperwork and, of course, interminable office battles over the dictionary's contents and even the meaning of specific words.

Company Speak must always give the appearance of being upbeat. It's meant to sanitize the ugly truth about the dysfunctional company and, of course, can't have any profanity either. For example, bullshit can be sent back to the bull, where it'll come out again as simply "excrement." A sentence might be something like, "That manager is full of excrement," thoroughly sanitized, yet still packing a punch, in a bureaucratic sense. It might still raise an eyebrow or two, if the hidden meaning is understood.

The Importance of Phony and Inflated Titles

Closely related to Company Speak is Title Creation. This is huge at dysfunctional companies. Properly mastered, Title Creation can cause tons of confusion. Titles should be long and have no bearing on what an employee actually does. Titles are also effective for fooling someone into thinking they've been promoted. Slight twists to a title, like the addition of words "Senior" or "Vice President" without any raises, direct reports or change in job description, gives the appearance of a promotion. This is the Principle of False Promotion Through Title Advancement (FPTTA – pronounced "FIP-tah," emphasis on the first syllable).

Dysfunctional companies are masters at FPTTA. Through sleight of hand, they tweak a title and, presto, the dazed employee's workload has doubled but with no raise, no staff and no real change in status.

There are two types of title inflation: Horizontal Title Inflation (HTI) and Vertical Title Inflation (VTI). In HTI, the employee stays in their same position, but their title expands to both the left and the right. In VTI, the employee may actually get promoted, and their title changes but remains only two or three words long.

A textbook example of Horizontal Title Inflation would be the following. Take someone who cleans toilets at the dysfunctional company's facility in Brooklyn. Said employee may start out with a title such as "Sanitation Engineer." Simply calling this particular employee "Cleaning Staff" is far too simple and obvious for the dysfunctional company. It just wouldn't be right. The dysfunctional company must stick to its mission of making the simple complicated.

Now, after some years of service, our Sanitation Engineer gets a promotion. This doesn't mean, of course, a change in the cleaning engineer's job. It still means cleaning toilets without additional staff. But the employee's clever manager took a course in Title Creation and FPTTA at the dysfunctional company's training institute and knows exactly what to do. The manager promotes the toilet cleaner to Senior Sanitation Engineer, a slight horizontal shift. Then after a few more years of cleaning toilets without help, the title gets changed to Senior Vice President Sanitation Engineer, another horizontal shift.

To make a long story short, eventually the title balloons, horizontally again, to Senior Vice President Sanitation Engineer Eastern Division. Since it isn't clear whether this is the eastern division of Brooklyn or Bangladesh, the title must be adjusted again after the next performance review to Senior Vice President Sanitation Engineer Eastern Division Domestic USA. At some point, our newly promoted toilet engineer will take more time to say his title than to clean the bathroom – another example of the dysfunctional company hard at work blocking productivity.

An example of the other type of title inflation, Vertical Title Inflation, might be the following:

An entry-level software developer might start out at the dysfunctional with the simple title "Developer." The dysfunctional company might instead call the newbie "Associate Developer," to give the false impression he has a long future with the company. After a few years toiling away on buggy applications, he becomes a "Senior Developer."

Then, one day, his supervisor, a rare manager who is at least semi-conscious, notices the high-quality work done by the Senior Developer and decides to make him a manager and give him staff. After a tortuous ritual with mounds of paperwork and an in-depth essay as long as a short novel, explaining why the employee should be promoted.

The management candidate was smart enough to put in the application package photos of himself recklessly partying with strangers in a bar during his summer vacation. It was the photo of him passed out face down on the floor that tipped the selection committee in his favor.

This is followed by an animal sacrifice in the parking lot, and then finally, the employee is reincarnated as Associate Development Manager.

Our newly minted manager now has several direct reports.

Since the supervisor is already called Development Manager, the underling can only be called Associate for now. The developer has actually made a move up the ladder, even though just one small rung, but the title has only been modified in one direction. This is an example of vertical inflation, an actual promotion in the hierarchy but only a small change in title.

Since this was only a small promotion, a squirrel or rabbit was sufficient for the animal sacrifice. For bigger promotions, or executive moves, a larger animal might need to be slaughtered and offered up to the Alter of Bureaucracy.

Then, as usually happens in the dysfunctional company, the Associate Development Manager's supervisor, the Development Manager, is the victim of a massive reorganization and is sent away never to be heard of again. The Associate Development Manager gets sucked up into the power vacuum and now replaces the Development Manager. Unfortunately, as luck would have it, our energetic new manager now reports to someone in accounting, who thinks software is a light jacket and that developers build buildings.

Thinking the Development Manager has too much overhead, his new accounting manager cuts his staff and he is back to being alone in the bureaucratic wilderness. Then, one day, the accounting manager gets axed, and the lonely developer has yet again another new clueless boss.

This doesn't faze our hero, at all, who has been through all of this before. Being a yo-yo, going up and down at random in the Hierarchy of Confusion is a way of life at the dysfunctional company.

Duplicate Name Reduction Program

A dysfunctional company might want to institute a **Duplicate Name Reduction Program (DNRP,** or DUN-rap) to reduce e-mail clutter. This program includes removing employees with duplicate names throughout the company.

For example, if there is a "Smith" in Purchasing, another one in Finance and maybe another in Scheduling, two will have to be let go. Even though their job roles don't overlap, and each serves a vital function in their department, they might accidentally get the same e-mail twice. This policy makes absolutely no sense and is, therefore, perfect for the dysfunctional company. It's another example of Habit One: If it makes sense, don't do it.

The Use of Company Speak at Home

The fully indoctrinated dysfunctional company employee may eventually start speaking Company Speak at home. Their bewildered family may not understand why they have to "pencil in" a dinner, or "schedule a placeholder" for lunch. Each meal will have "takeaways" – not to be confused with carry out or leftovers – each family member must complete before the next meal.

The question is whether the buzzed-out employee's family will have "bandwidth" to assign "resources" for proper "execution" of the task or will have a "missed opportunity." If this continues, the family might want to seek professional help or join a support group for families with employees of dysfunctional companies.

Seeking Outside Help and Next Steps

In rare lucid moments, when someone might actually use common sense, speak clearly or try to simplify things, the dysfunctional company can always turn to outsiders to slow things down. Here, a corollary of the basic rule applies: To err is human; to really confuse things takes an outside consultant as already explained in Habit One.

As has been seen, e-mail serves not only as a tool for the dysfunctional company to miscommunicate and disinform, it also serves as a business blocker. The next habit covers its twin in the BBT duet – meetings.

Habit Four:
If You're Not in A Meeting,
You Will Be Assigned to One

"I knew I should've brought my vomit bags.
I got queasy as soon as the meeting started."

If You're Not in A Meeting,
You Will Be Assigned to One

"My psychiatrist said I would get better,
if I had fewer meetings."

Employees should be in meetings as much of the work day as possible.

Excessive meeting attendance serves two purposes in the dysfunctional company. It gives the appearance that real work is actually getting done (again, **The Principle of the Appearance of Activity**), and it ties up employees in unproductive activities for long periods of time.

Meetings should be long and boring, even pointless, with no real conclusion. An inconclusive meeting, of course, requires another meeting, maybe even the formation of another committee or working group. Meetings beget meetings in an endless cycle of unproductivity. Meetings should run consecutively, allowing employees to move seamlessly between meetings without a break.

The key thing is that it is far more important to plan until paralysis than to actually get anything done. Along with excessive e-mails, which was covered in Habit Three, meeting attendance is the perfect prescription for company inertia. For more information about weekly meetings, or TWMs, a special species of meeting, refer to Habit One, where this is covered in detail.

Employees have been known to disappear in meeting black holes, never to be heard of again. Concerned coworkers might ask a manager about the whereabouts of a colleague, who hasn't been seen in months, only to be told that the employee has been in meetings. When told the employee's name was in the obituaries, the manager will reply that although people have been known to drop dead in company meetings, this never happens at "our" company. This hopefully will calm any concerns among coworkers about the fate of the missing employee.

Meetings are the ideal platform for the cast of characters who make the company dysfunctional to display their talents proudly out in the open – ego maniacs, political powerheads, blowhards, loudmouths, non-stop talkers, grand standers, show offs, boring policy wonks, gloom and doom naysayers, and overbearing jerks and micromanagers.

Employees can attend meetings either in person, such as in a meeting room, or by dialing in from their desk or, in the case of remote employees, from a location outside the office. Some employees who frequently dial in to meetings may opt for having their headphones surgically attached to their head. This is much easier than constantly putting on and taking off uncomfortable headphones. Ideally, even without surgery, the employee shouldn't need to remove headphones, since he or she should always be in a meeting.

Employees walking around the office with headphones, either surgically attached or just atop their head, is a common sight in the dysfunctional office. **Headphone Removal Anxiety** is also a common ailment among employees at the dysfunctional company.

The Key Role of the Meeting Police (MP): Keeping Employees in Meetings

Meeting attendance should be enforced by the company **Meeting Police (MP)**. MPs are full-time employees whose sole job is to patrol the halls, looking for stray employees who might not be in a meeting. MPs are dressed in accordance with the company's dress code (for example, suit and tie, business casual or Bermuda shorts and flip flops). They can be identified by their armbands, clearly marked MP.

When an MP sees an employee in the hall, he or she will approach the employee and ask if the employee is in a meeting, or on their way to a meeting. If the employee answers affirmative, the employee will be expected to give the meeting name, time and location. The employee will be expected to provide proof of the meeting before being allowed to pass. Evidence that the meeting exists can consist of either a print out of an e-mail or meeting invitation or a display of such information on a phone or laptop.

If the employee is unable to provide such evidence, or admits to not being in a meeting, the MP will then find a meeting, even if it has nothing to do with the employee's job function, and assign the employee to that meeting. The MP will have a list of all meetings in progress at the company, and their locations, on either a clip board or tablet, depending on the level of technology at the company. The MP will then handcuff and escort the unassigned employee to their newly assigned meeting.

After the meeting, during one of those rare moments when time isn't assigned to a meeting, the employee is expected to return immediately to their PAWS to await further instructions or assignment to a new meeting.

The only exception to this rule should be for auditors. As the secret police of the company, auditors are free to roam throughout the premises at will. They may show up at any moment to arrest an unsuspecting employee guilty of even the smallest infraction of some obscure company policy. They may knock on the door of a meeting in progress, or even be sitting under cover in plainclothes in the meeting itself. They may even be crouched under the table, trying to camouflage themselves as floor tiles or carpeting.

Employees need to be extra careful of auditors hidden in meetings.

When approached by an MP, an auditor will pull out their yellow identity card, which is clearly marked "AUDITOR" in large capital letters. This allows the auditor to pass freely through any MP checkpoint in the hall.

Remote employees, out of sight of MPs, pose a challenge to this policy. Remote employees should have monitoring software on their laptops that can detect when they're dialed into a meeting. If they're not dialed into a meeting, the software should display a flashing and annoying pop-up window that blocks the employee from doing anything else on the laptop. The software should then scan the meeting in progress list – a virtual MP, if you will – and automatically dial the employee into a meeting, again, even if it's completely unrelated to the employee's job.

The virtual MP seizes the employee's laptop and takes control, just like the physical MP in the office.

The Two Types of Meetings: Packed and Unpacked

There are two types of meetings at the dysfunctional company: **Packed**, or Structured meetings and **Unpacked** or Unstructured meetings.

A Packed meeting, as the name implies, has a totally packed schedule. The meeting leader has a dizzying list of items to cover, one right after the other in rapid succession with no break. Usually, the meeting leader has knowledge of the subject matter, and knows exactly what he or she wants to accomplish. This is rare at the dysfunctional company, but it does happen.

The agenda is so tight, meeting participants don't have time for bio breaks. In the absence of bio breaks, the meeting leader should issue buckets for attendees to easily relieve themselves under the table without having to get up.

Meeting participants may also get dizzy from too much information being thrown at them at once and may suddenly pass out. Smelling salts should be a part of the emergency first-aid kit in every meeting room for these situations.

This is just the first phase of what is known as **Acute Meeting Psychosis (AMP**, pronounced "amp" like the electrical unit). In more advanced stages, meeting participants may bang their head against the table, have a heart attack or stop breathing altogether.

The emergency first-aid kit in every meeting room of the dysfunctional company should contain the following items:

1. Smelling salts
2. Gauze bandages and cotton balls
3. Defibrillator
4. Oxygen tanks

Smelling salts, as just discussed, are for the first phase of AMP. The gauze bandages are used to wrap the heads of attendees banging their heads on the table, and the cotton balls are for nose bleeds, also common in second stage AMP. The defibrillator is for attendees who get heart attacks in third-degree AMP.

There may be times, more common in Packed than Unpacked meetings, where a shocking announcement is made. Most attendees may just gasp, but those not in the company health plan may stop breathing altogether and require oxygen tanks to be resuscitated.

Unpacked or Unstructured Meetings . . .

Unpacked meetings are the norm at the dysfunctional company. They're completely disorganized – the polar opposite of a Packed meeting. The agenda, if there is one, is set by the meeting leader, who may or may not be competent to conduct the meeting. Discussion should flow aimlessly with no purpose or clear focus. The agenda is just a guide that can, and usually, be ignored.

Unpacked meetings start with the meeting leader asking if anybody has any knowledge or expertise of the matter at hand. Those answering yes should be immediately excused from the meeting. This will guarantee no relevant discussion takes place.

Next, the meeting leader may optionally ask participants if they're wearing their underwear with the company logo. A show of hands is sufficient. Since HR rules prevent employees from exposing their underwear during meetings, verification of compliance is on the honor system.

An employee brave enough to admit they're wearing their lucky underwear, which doesn't have a company logo, should be removed from the meeting immediately. The meeting leader should call security and have the offending employee taken to HR for punishment for violating the

Company Underwear Policy (CUP). Audit, of course, should also be notified, as a backup.

The CUP cleared away, and anybody with expertise excused, the unproductive meeting can now proceed.

The Proper Course for All Meetings

All meetings, whether Packed or Unpacked, should follow the same pattern. The door to the meeting room must be closed and clearly marked that the room is occupied. Remote employees should have the desktop icon on their laptop change color, a red circle with a diagonal bar is recommended, indicating they're in a meeting and can't be disturbed.

Of course, in the dysfunctional company, where multitasking is the norm, as was seen in Habit Two, people will still try to reach the employee, whether remote or onsite, via IM or chat or whatever technical intrusion device the company is using. This will help keep the employee distracted and unengaged in the meeting and waffling around, juggling several tasks simultaneously in accordance with The Principal of the Appearance of Activity.

Meeting participants should be encouraged to speak their minds, even if it has nothing to do with the topic of the meeting. Some may go off on tangents or down rabbit holes. Others, particularly those with strong personalities, may try to hijack the meeting for their own purposes, in a meeting coup d'état. They may try to rile up attendees, bringing up common complaints, which employees are embarrassed to discuss, such as the lack of toilet paper in the bathrooms or the frequent outbreaks of Salmonella from the food in the cafeteria.

Behavior in meetings should follow strict guidelines set by HR. Participants should be allowed to speak out freely, even cut off, or talk, over each other. Healthy disagreements should be allowed to escalate, even fester, into verbal feuds. Shouting matches, punctuated by bouts of screaming and yelling, are common.

HR rules for meetings allow employees to verbally abuse each other, as long as they're civil. In practice, this means, anything goes, as long as obscenities, or lewd hand gestures, aren't used. However, comparing a coworker to a barnyard animal is acceptable, as long as it's said with respect and dignity.

Meetings are also the ideal forum to publicly humiliate employees. Managers can openly attack salespeople who haven't meet their quota. Employees with interesting or creative ideas can be belittled by both management and their co-workers. Everybody else can take potshots at anybody else for not wearing the latest clothing style or missing some obscure pop culture reference or sports game on TV the night before.

At some point, the meeting leader has to intervene and put an end to the circus. The most effective tool for doing so is the PowerPoint presentation. In fact, company policy should require the use of PowerPoint in every meeting. **Death by PowerPoint (DBPP**, pronounced "DEE-bip," the emphasis on the "DEE") is a frequent theme of many meetings in the dysfunctional company.

PowerPoint is always preferred over whiteboards.

Whiteboards encourage open thinking and creativity and, as a result, have no place in dysfunctional meetings. Besides, when meeting attendees start heated arguments and start swearing or yelling at each other – very common in dysfunctional meetings – attendees may use the markers as weapons, or try to mark up their opponent's clothing with obscene symbols.

When it's obvious the meeting is going nowhere, the meeting leader should blow a whistle, dim the lights and start the obligatory PowerPoint presentation. The presentation should use every feature of PowerPoint – blinking letters, flying banners, pictures fading in and out, colored arrows shooting across the screen in all directions and annoying sound effects. Meeting participants then pull out their company-issued laser pointers, pointing at random at the screen, in a sort of sound and light show.

If power goes out during the meeting, caused by a burnt-out laptop from too many PowerPoint presentations going on simultaneously in the room, finger puppets and hand shadow plays are an allowed substitute.

Meeting participants may experience a range of emotions during the meeting. The most common are crying outbursts or fits of uncontrollable laughter. There are many things in the meeting that may also cause participants to feel queasy or nauseous. Employees should refrain from throwing up.

Vomiting in meetings is bad form, even for a dysfunctional company, and should be discouraged. Just in case, every employee should pack a company-issued vomit bag along with their laser pointer in their laptop bag as part of their meeting survival kit. The company might also want to offer a mandatory course in nausea management to their repertoire of useless and unnecessary training. Attendance at such training, of course, should be noted in the employee's annual performance review.

Eventually, meeting participants will start to pass out or get bored, since no clear objective came out of the meeting. At this point, another follow-up meeting should be scheduled, and the meeting should be adjourned. Participants may smile, or pat each other on the back, if this type of touching is allowed by HR, as they leave the meeting, more out of relief that the ordeal is over than out of a sense of accomplishment.

Since nausea occurs so frequently in meetings, a brief detour on the proper use of vomit bags is in order.

Vomit Bag Procedures for Meetings

Whenever an employee starts to feel queasy during a meeting, they should ask to be excused. They should immediately reach for a vomit bag in their company-issued duffle bag and proceed to the nearest exit. Ideally, the employee should head to the nearest bathroom. If they don't make it, at least, they have the vomit bag at hand.

If they only get as far as the hall, they should seal up the vomit bag after use and hand it to the nearest MP. The MP will properly dispose of the vomit bag in company-approved sanitation facilities, often located next to food being prepared in the kitchen in the cafeteria.

To avoid nosy auditors, company-issued vomit bags are preferred. If the employee only has airline vomit bags, they should make sure the bags conform to the **Company Issued Vomit Bag Standard**.

Well-prepared employees carry their supply of vomit bags around with them all day in their company duffle bag as they go from meeting to meeting. Remote employees keep their duffle bag handy at their side next to their remote PAWS.

Duffle bags with the company logo are standard equipment for all employees and are issued during **New Hire Disorientation**. These duffle bags include items needed for daily survival, such as water bottles and laser pointers, both for use, like vomit bags, during meetings.

Other duffle bag items the employee may add for marathon meetings include snacks, especially those that are crunchy and annoying, sedatives and bandages, in case the employee might try to hurt themselves.

New Hire Disorientation and duffle bags are discussed in detail in Habit Six about employees.

Remote Employees Must Be Clothed at All Times

Since remote employees are required to attend meetings, they must also follow company meeting etiquette whether dialing in or attending by video conference or Zoom. Remote employees play just as crucial a role in meetings as their office-imprisoned colleagues. Modern technology can make them feel like they're part of the action. They can feel the same pain without being physically present.

They may not have to endure being packed into a smelly conference room with no ventilation, and with people they can't stand, or forced to drink nauseating refreshments, but, at least, they must still be clothed at all times, just like their office colleagues.

People wouldn't come naked to meetings in the office, right? Not normally, unless it was required as part of some forced socializing event. The same goes for remote employees.

It's also unacceptable for remote employees to wear pajamas, bathrobes or only underwear on web cams or during video meetings an Zoom calls.

Remote employees observed, either partially or fully, unclad may be summoned to HR, virtually, of

175

course, and may be the subject of an audit finding for violating the **Remote Employee Undress Code** (the infamous "**REUC**," pronounced REE-ook, emphasis on the "REE").

After being disciplined, pictures of the offending employee should be posted on an internal company web site, where other employees can body shame them, or post indecent comments.

Crafty employees have been known to end run this policy by wearing only a shirt or top and no pants or skirt or anything else below the waist. These employees should be careful not to stand up during meetings, so their ruse won't be exposed.

Kids and pets are exempt from this policy and are encouraged to appear on screen at key points in a meeting. Their presence shouldn't be considered a disruption but a way to move the action forward at sluggish meetings.

Screaming kids can provide their insight into the subject being discussed, and pets, particularly barking dogs, can express approval or disapproval. If the matter at hand is idiotic, often the case in meetings at dysfunctional companies, screaming kids and barking dogs are just as intelligent as what the grownups and humans in the meeting have to say.

A really useful pet for remote meetings is the family ferret. The ferret can signal its thoughts on a proposal. After every response, it should be given a candy wrapped with the company logo. If the ferret is sniffing at the screen, it likes the idea, and it should move forward. If the ferret yawns, the whole thing is stupid and should be sent back to be updated. If the ferret lifts its leg and pisses on the screen, the proposal should be rejected immediately, no questions asked.

The Importance of Team Building Exercises

Another type of pointless meeting is the team building exercise. Dysfunctional companies often have these at annual company events outside the office. These are often held in out-of-the-way locations like Las Vegas, Paris, Dubai, Hong Kong or Rio de Janeiro where there are few distractions and employees can focus on the planned events. Company events are the perfect excuse for excessive drinking and carousing, and all attendees should be coerced into participating, whether they drink or not.

Since no productive work is actually being conducted at the dysfunctional company during the rest of the year, the loss of a week at an offsite event doesn't make a difference. The team building exercise can just be added to the already long list of time-wasting activities at the dysfunctional company.

Team building exercises may include driving bumper cars, roller derbies, being stuck by Velcro to a wall or paintball contests, all of which teach skills absolutely vital for work in the dysfunctional office. A novel idea is to send the entire team to survival training in Antarctica. Inevitably, some participants may not come back in a Darwinian thinning of the employee herd. This shouldn't pose a staffing problem. Employees in the dysfunctional company are disposable, anyways, and can be easily replaced or backfilled by HR.

The Key Metric for Meeting Attendance: Meeting Attendance Ratios

It should be noted that strict meeting attendance increases the employee's **Meeting Attendance Ratios (MARs)**, always a major goal in annual performance reviews.

This follows the common practice at dysfunctional companies of reducing every employee activity, and the employees themselves, in fact, to a metric. Numbers are far more important than people, and slavish worship of metrics is more important than intuition and common sense.

The Goal: The Paralysis of Meeting Nirvana

Successful implementation of this habit will result in **Meeting Nirvana**, where everybody everywhere in the company is attending a meeting somewhere at the same time. At this point, all productive activity ceases, and the dysfunctional company completely shuts down until power is restored.

Habit Five:
Human Contact with Customers Is Prohibited

"Help the customer?
We weren't trained for that."

Habit Five:
Human Contact with Customers Is Prohibited

"It's not my job.
Let me forward you over to someone
*who really **can't** help you."*

Customers are annoying.

They complain and whine about the product or service, and then have the nerve to suggest improvements. They may try to contact the company directly by phone or e-mail or chat to make complaints. They may even dare to contact the company for after-sales support and service.

This is totally unacceptable and must be stopped immediately. There should be as little human contact as possible between employees and customers. Employees should never be allowed to interact directly with customers. Employees caught talking to customers should be disciplined, or subject to audit findings, and all incidents should be noted as a negative item in their performance review.

This habit only applies to employees, and their internal support staff, who provide, or are supposed to provide, service or disservice, as is usually the case, to customers, after the product or service has been sold and delivered to the customer.

This habit doesn't apply to salespeople, for example, who have to interact with potential, or existing, customers to make the sale. It also doesn't apply to employees at companies who provide services directly to customers or clients like professional services – legal, accounting and consulting, for example – or product services, such as installation, maintenance, and transportation of equipment and goods.

Of course, the rest of the employees at the dysfunctional company who have no reason to talk to customers should also be barred from doing so. They should be shielded from customers by any means possible. Barbed wire fences, locked doors and thick sound-proof walls are all examples of effective tools for shielding the other employees from customers. Their contacts, as well, with outsiders should be carefully monitored and subject to audit review and punishment by HR.

How to Keep Customers from Reaching the Company

Customers attempting to contact the company for assistance should be given the run-around and transferred from department to department with their questions unanswered. Helping customers wastes valuable time employees could be using for other unproductive activities, like office politics or creating new acronyms.

Employees need to be left alone to attend meetings, shuffle paper in search of endless approvals, play bureaucratic games and office politics, and appear busy while doing nothing. Trying to serve customers, or outright pretending to serve them, if this habit is applied correctly, also gets in the way of forced socializing, which always takes precedence over any work, or attempt at work.

Customers interfere with all these activities.

Remember the twin enemies of the dysfunctional company: its customers and its employees. This habit will discuss customer abuse and the next habit will cover the poor treatment of employees.

Just as Habit Three was about the use of poor communication to keep employees off base, this habit is about using poor marketing to keep customers confused. Besides poor, or non-existent, customer service at the dysfunctional company, poor marketing communication is necessary to keep customers off base. This is all part of the whole poor service and marketing experience provided by the dysfunctional company.

So, while Habit Three is about poor internal communications, this habit is about poor external communication.

Three Rules of Customer Mistreatment:

1) **The customer is the enemy.**
2) **The customer is always wrong.**
3) **If a customer has a question, see Rule #1**

The attitude of the dysfunctional company is, "You bought it. It's yours. We can't help you. Go away. You're on your own. We don't provide support." Just being upfront and saying, "We don't care about you. You're screwed," or even only, "We don't care, period," would be too obvious. The dysfunctional company isn't about clear communication to its customers.

The dysfunctional company uses two tactics for irritating customers and making sure they never get any assistance – the **Clean Desk Policy** and **Customer Disservice**.

Customers should be made to feel small and insignificant. They should feel like they're just another face in the crowd. Not unique. Not special. The subliminal message is: "We don't need your business."

This is the goal of **Customer Disservice**.

The Clean Desk Policy

On the surface, the **Clean Desk Policy** is for security. It makes sense that sensitive documents shouldn't be sitting exposed on desks, physical or virtual, for the world to see. In the dysfunctional company, it isn't about common sense. This policy has an ulterior motive beside security, since security isn't top of mind for the dysfunctional company.

The Clean Desk Policy is the internal procedure for handling a customer issue after it has gotten past – if it can even get through – **Customer Teleabuse** to Customer Disservice. In short, Customer Disservice is the external face of the dysfunctional company to customers, and the Clean Desk Policy is the ugly internal procedures inside the company that the customer never sees. Customer Disservice is external, while the Clean Desk Policy is internal.

The Clean Desk Policy requires employees to have a "clean" desktop, meaning no paperwork or other work-related documents must be on their desktop. This "desktop" could be either the physical desktop at their PAWS, or the virtual desktop on their laptop screen.

In practice, the Clean Desk Policy turns the dysfunctional company into a conveyor belt. Work moves down the conveyor belt from desk to desk. The purpose of this game is for employees to make sure nothing sits on their desk – ever. Anything that crosses their desk must be moved to another desk. The conveyor belt must be kept moving.

The first words an employee must say when something lands on their desk is, "It's not my department," or "It's not my job," and then proceed to move it on to the next employee in the chain. From there, the next employee repeats the procedure, also explaining that it's not their department or job, and then moves the issue to the next link on the conveyor belt – the next employee in line – and so on forever.

Eventually, there is no one at the end of the conveyor belt to handle the matter. The issue mysteriously disappears into thin air, never to be heard of again. It fell into the black hole on the clean desk.

An automatically generated e-mail from Customer Disservice should then be sent to the customer. The e-mail should say the matter has been resolved. The e-mail shouldn't just come out and clearly say the issue has been resolved. It should use convoluted language to keep the customer sufficiently confused but still hint everything has been taken care of.

The e-mail should come from an anonymous mailbox that can't receive replies and shouldn't have any contact person, e-mail or phone number where any questions can be directed. This will achieve this habit's goal to distance the company further from the customer.

The Clean Desk Policy effectively keeps not only employees – but also customers – clean by magically making their complaints disappear.

As with every policy at the dysfunctional company, whether large and small, compliance is subject to review by audit followed by its corresponding punishments of brutal interrogation, excessive findings, and banishment and exile to training in company correction camps.

Before the matter could even be digested by the dysfunctional company to be mashed up and spit out, it had to be received from an aggrieved customer. This is the function of Customer Disservice.

Keeping Customers Unhappy: The Vital Function of Customer Disservice

Customer Disservice should be a rat's nest of messed up and lost orders, misdirected communications, ignored customer requests, phantom orders ("I never ordered that.") and lost shipments and missed appointments. It should be totally automated to avoid the horrifying scenario of an employee actually having to talk directly to a customer, though this isn't always possible.

The best way to play hide-and-seek with customers is to route their calls through a voicemail jungle. The best voice mailboxes are anonymous and unattended, never heard by a human being. Some should already be full and can't take any more calls. The caller shouldn't be aware, of course, the mailbox is already full and should be lured into leaving a message by a reassuring announcement – something along the lines of "Your call is important to us. Please leave a message, and we'll get back to you as soon as possible."

Little do they know; no employee will ever get back to them, because no employee ever gets their message. It vaporizes into bureaucratic outer space as soon as it's received.

Product defects and service failures are the norm at the dysfunctional company. The product never works as promised, or advertised, and isn't easy to use and requires support. The same for services, which are rarely delivered on time or to the level of quality promised. Where does the customer turn? Who else, **Customer Disservice**, of course? There is no other option. The dance begins.

The Teleabuse Tango:
The Dance with Customer Disservice

The journey to customer dissatisfaction begins when the customer tries to find out how to contact the company. This usually starts with the "Contact Us" link, if there is one, on the company web site. There should only be a link to a generic e-mail address or to a page with text fields, where a message can be entered, then submitted, hopefully, to someone at the company. Who knows? It could be just another empty mailbox, like the Customer Disservice voicemail system, lost in cyberspace, never to be heard of again. The whole experience should be cold and impersonal, leaving the customer feeling anonymous and unimportant.

Under no circumstances should the phone number for Customer Disservice be on the company web site. It should be impossible to find. The dysfunctional company's web site is normally unnavigable, itself just another source of many customer complaints, making it easy to conceal any way to contact anyone helpful. Even if the customer could reach someone at the company, they would probably be clueless.

It should take extensive searching online to find the Customer Disservice phone number, iffy at best, since the number might not even exist. Assuming the customer finds the coveted phone number, in some hidden web site on the Dark Web, they can begin their Quixotic quest for assistance.

Before starting, the customer needs to understand that Customer Disservice is flooded with calls, due to the large number of unhappy customers trying to reach the company. Phone lines often are backed up for hours.

The Typical Pattern of Calls to Customer Disservice

A typical call should follow a predictable pattern. Customer Teleabuse begins the moment the disgruntled customer calls in and is greeted with an automated answering system. These systems should be a maze with no escape. The customer is presented with a dizzying menu of choices, none of which are exactly what they're looking for. The bewildered customer then picks something, anything – they have to do something in order to move to the next menu – descending deeper into menu chaos. The next menu is more of the same, another bunch of confusing choices, still not exactly what the customer is looking for.

Each menu choice should lead to another menu, and then another menu after that, and so on, ad infinitum. No menu option should ever allow the customer to talk to a human being. The only escape hatch should be an option to return to the main menu to start the whole process over again. Sometimes, if the caller hits the right sequence of numbers they win **Menu Bingo** and actually get an intelligent response. Menus should be designed to ensure this doesn't happen often.

If the system is working properly the desired outcome should be that the customer hangs up or throws the phone against the wall. The dysfunctional company will have effectively again used Customer Teleabuse to achieve its goal of keeping customers away from employees.

A nice feature of some of these systems, designed to enhance the customer experience, is voice recognition. Instead of dialing the number of the menu item, the customer is asked to say their choice in a few words. The system shouldn't understand their voice. It should respond, "I'm sorry. I didn't get that. Let's try again." The caller is then forced back into the menu. If the customer tries to speak again, the system still shouldn't understand. This should continue in an infinite feedback loop that always goes back to the same menu. In fact, the system should be designed to never respond to any human voice, at all.

If the customer is already pissed off, voice recognition will just push them over the edge. This is Customer Teleabuse at its best.

Another dodge to keep customers at bay on automated phone systems is to require they can only enter a number – an account or bill number, for example – to proceed. The system is totally automated. When the customer calls in, the first, and only, thing it asks for is an account number. If the customer doesn't have an account yet, or is trying to set up a new account, or is calling about something other than their account or bill, such as a question about their product or service, they're screwed. They can't enter anything besides a number, since this is the only input the menu will accept. This will stonewall even the peskiest of customers.

Some intrepid customers will fight back. They will try to reach a human being at any cost. Some customers will bang repeatedly on the Operator key, or just keep screaming, "REPRESENTATIVE," "HELP," or "MAY DAY," into the phone at the top of their lungs. The system may respond with the usual, "I'm sorry. I didn't understand that," and hang up, or it may finally transfer the call. Also yelling obscenities has been known to be effective in trying to reach a human.

If they're lucky, their call is answered by a live – and this is questionable, signs of breathing should be heard first – Customer Disservice representative.

If they're unlucky, the line will ring non-stop and then suddenly go dead. The customer tries to call again. This time the customer enters the magic kingdom, and there is an answer, not by a human being, but a recorded message: "You're call is important to us. Someone should be with you shortly." Then there is a dramatic pause, the line may go silent for a minute, followed by another ghost message: "Your estimated wait time is," then another pause as a computer-generated voice, not quite in synch with the rest of the recorded message, says, "five minutes."

The wait time, of course, is complete nonsense. Customers have been known to wait for hours until someone answers the call. It's a good idea to pack a meal and bring something to drink, preferably alcoholic, before starting the call. In the meantime, the customer is entertained by mind-numbing music – the best is obnoxious and repetitive banging noises – interspersed every few minutes with the same recorded message, saying someone will be with them shortly, or some other lie how their call is important to the company. Sometimes there is a pause, and it sounds like someone is about to come on the line. No chance. The music and recorded message return with a vengeance, like a bad headache.

Another popular Teleabuse trick, to make the customer think an answer is imminent, is to add a dial-back feature. After the wait time is announced, the system will ask the caller if they want to be called back. The customer is promised that their place in line will be kept, if they just provide a call back number. The customer naively leaves a number, hangs up and, as expected, is forgotten and never called back. This is called Customer Deterrence (CD) and should be employed as much as possible as another tactic to keep prying customers away.

How Customer Disservice Should Poorly Handle Live Calls

In the unlikely event the customer actually reaches someone in Customer Disservice, their problems are only beginning.

The Customer Disservice representative should always be reading from a script. They should be given a thick book with tons of scripts to choose from. No impromptu conversation should be allowed, at all. Every question has a stock answer from which the representative must not veer. The representative should always sound like they're reading from a book. Nothing should ever sound natural.

Answers should be cryptic and unclear, much like the internal communication within the dysfunctional company. Customers should be humiliated with responses like, "Don't you know?" and "That's our company policy." Customer Disserve representatives should be aloof and defensive. "What do you mean it doesn't work?" It's essential for effective Teleabuse to establish an adversarial relationship with the customer as early as possible in the conversation.

The dysfunctional company may require disservice representatives to ask, "To whom do I have the pleasure of speaking today?" The customer should never fall for this ruse. The representative isn't pleased and is probably pissed off to have to talk to someone. The customer is probably disturbing the representative's nap time.

Customer Disservice representatives can also duck answering a question with, "Read the documentation on the web site," or "Did you check the documentation on the web site first, before calling?" Another customer avoidance technique is for the representative just to say, "You could have done that online. There's no need to call us." The customer may be calling, because they've already tried to read the documentation, which is incomprehensible, or because the web site doesn't work, or has gone down, often the case at the dysfunctional company.

If the representative finds that none of their scripts answer the customer's question, they shouldn't be allowed to ad lib. They should never be allowed to make up an answer, especially if it's their own. Creativity is prohibited. They should take one of the scripts at random, even if completely unrelated to the question, and read it back to the customer. This continues the cycle of confusion created during the call.

The customer should be left wondering why they bothered to call in the first place. The name of the game is Blame the Customer. It's their fault. They just don't understand the product or service, and the Customer Disservice representative isn't about to teach them. The attitude is that the customer is stupid. They just don't know how to use the product or service correctly.

If the representative gets really lost, which happens often, they can put the customer on hold and transfer the call. "It's not my department. Let me forward your call." This can also be employed if the customer asks to speak to a manager or gets surly. The music and recorded messages should come back. After waiting for another eternity, a new representative should come on the line. This representative shouldn't have any idea why the customer is calling. He or she shouldn't have been forwarded any details from the previous representative. The customer is forced to repeat their sad story from the beginning.

Unless the customer specifically asks to speak to a manager, the representative should never transfer the call to a manager or supervisor. This only invites trouble for the representative, who might have to admit they made a mistake to their superior. Then again, this being the dysfunctional company, both the representative and his or her manager are probably idiots. In that case, it doesn't matter with whom the customer is speaking. Everything will still always go south.

The customer should be made to feel there is no way out. They should feel like they're trapped in a zoo, where everybody is a monkey, wherever they turn.

Customer Disservice is just like the rest of the dysfunctional company. Representatives shouldn't be doing any productive work. Whenever a representative receives a call, they should transfer it immediately, without listening to it, to the next representative, who, in turn, moves it to the next representative, and so on. Just like other employees at the dysfunctional company, Customer Disservice representatives are moving down a conveyor belt on an assembly line. Eventually, like musical chairs, there aren't any more chairs to receive calls, and no calls get answered.

This fits in perfectly with the Customer Disservice model, where customers are shunted from representative to representative with no resolution of their problem. The daisy chain should end in an offshore call center with someone speaking in an unintelligible foreign accent. The call center should be in a noisy crowded office. The chatter of other representatives in the background should almost drown out the call. The representative should be using the same scripts as all the prior representatives. The customer will finally figure out, they're being fed the same garbage all over again, this time in a foreign accent.

The Proper Use of Technology to Keep Customer Away

An alternative to automated phone systems are chatbots. The chatbot is ideal for Customer Disservice, because it doesn't require human contact with the customer. In fact, it isn't even human.

A chatbot is a cute little blinking icon in the lower right-hand corner of the company web site that the customer can use to chat with an employee, supposedly. The chatbot might have a thumbnail of someone's face and a name. The customer thinks they're talking to a real human being. They have no idea they're really having a conversation with a computer.

The alert customer shouldn't be fooled. They're not chatting with an actual employee, at all, but a computer-generated fake human. The photo isn't of a real person. It's a headshot downloaded from a glamor magazine or porn web site.

The chatbot window then opens and might say something like, "Hi, this is Suzie. How can I help you today?" Suzie looks and sounds like real, but she doesn't exist. Her name was just pulled out of thin air from a computer and strapped onto the bot to make it look real. Suzie the bot is just a figment of the customer's imagination, mimicking live Customer Disservice representatives and belching out their same nonsensical scripts.

Ultimately, Suzie is as worthless as her live counterparts. She can't help, or answer the question, and then randomly posts a generic message in the chat window, saying the matter has been resolved. The chatbot, in true dysfunctional style, shuts down, disappears and can't be retrieved by the customer. The whole experience should be surreal to the customer.

Technology is a double-edged sword. It can streamline and make service easier for the customer. Not so for the dysfunctional company. Technology is another weapon to isolate customers and keep them away from the company. Systems for contacting the company should be complicated and hard to use, if and when they work, to hopefully, drive away nosy customers.

The words "streamline" and "easier," or "user-friendly," aren't in the twisted vocabulary of the dysfunctional company. User-friendly? No way. More like, "stay away," "keep off the grass," or "stop bothering me." Another good one is "You again? Didn't you call yesterday about the same thing?" The representative is implying, "Are you so stupid you couldn't have figured it out by now." This is another example of the fine art of Teleabuse.

Social media should also be used extensively to keep customers from interacting directly with the company. Instead of a contact number or e-mail, a bunch of icons for every social media platform in the universe should be at the bottom of the web site. This leaves the customer confused as to which social media platform to use. It doesn't really matter, since they're all equally bad at reaching anybody at the company for help. Besides being on the least visible part of the web site, the string of icons should be as small as possible to make them hard to see and even harder to click on.

In addition, if customers get really nasty, marketing people in charge of the dysfunctional company's social media accounts can just block negative customers. Marketing can even post fake positive comments under phony names. Nothing is too low for the dysfunctional company.

It's inevitable a persistent and annoying customer will reach a Customer Disservice representative. Disservice representatives can only hide for so long behind company walls. Eventually, every Customer Disservice representative gets hit. When this happens, they must still make sure to completely follow Teleabuse procedures with all customers. No customer should ever be spared the full wrath of Teleabuse.

Since talking to customers is against company policy, every customer contact must be logged and added to the representative's **Customer Acceptance Ratio (CAR)**. This ratio is calculated as the percentage of live calls with customers divided by the total number of calls received by the representative. Ideally, the dysfunctional company strives for a zero CAR. Since mistakes happen and some customers still break through the virtual barbed wire and trenches, there will always be some CAR. CARs are periodically reviewed by audit to make sure they stay low and are a big part of every disservice representative's annual performance review.

Customer Disservice Offices:
Customer Disservice In-Person

If the dysfunctional company requires a physical presence or office for Customer Disservice representatives for its product or service, special precautions must be taken to shield employees from customers.

Customer Disservice representatives should be behind heavy bullet proof glass, which should be smoked or heavily tinted to hide the identity of employees. This also protects employees from irate customers who might try to jump over counters and strangle employees. All communication should be through speakers in the glass that alter the representative's voice for further protection. The speakers should be scratchy, requiring customers and representatives to yell at other.

There should be no receptionists at company facilities. Visitors should enter an empty foyer with just a phone next to a locked door. For added effect, a security camera over the door should be peering down on the visitor, making the visit as intimidating and unwelcoming as possible.

If a reception area with live humans is required, it should be on a perch looking down on visitors, reinforcing their unimportance to the dysfunctional company. Receptionists should take down the visitor's name, the time of their appointment and the name of the employee they're visiting. They should then be escorted to a seat in the lobby and left there in limbo. The visitor should never be given any clue as to the status of their appointment, and the response to any request for information should be, "We're working on it."

Customer Disservice, whether by phone, by chat, or in person, or even social media, is one of the great mysteries of the dysfunctional universe, unseen and unknowable. To the customer, the dysfunctional company is just an impersonal blob out of reach and out of touch, and not accountable for its products and services.

In the rare instance a customer finds a helpful – and knowledgeable – Customer Disservice agent, they should keep their contact information for dear life. They may have to use smoke signals or covert communication channels to get back to their beloved Customer Disservice rep in the future, but it's worthwhile if there is any hope of getting help.

In Customer Disservice, it pays to have friends in low places.

The Special Case of Retail Establishments

If the dysfunctional company has retail outlets, special rules are required to reduce customer contact. There should be as few salespeople on the floor as possible. The outlet should be understaffed, leaving customers to wander around looking for help. When a customer sees a salesperson, they should already be busy with another customer and can't be bothered.

Ideally, salespeople should be replaced by automated kiosks with lighted arrows on the floor, directing customers where their merchandise is located. If the product happens to be in the back, the kiosk should send a message to a salesperson hiding in the warehouse, who pops out from a side door and hands the product to the customer and walks away. The salesperson should walk away before the customer can ask a question.

Before disappearing, the salesperson should grunt something about paying for the merchandise and point to the cashier.

The cashier, as well, should be behind a checkout lane and cash register, beyond reach of the customer, and only be allowed to say numbers. Friendly conversation, or anything making the customer feel welcome at the store, must not be allowed.

The cashier should only be able to say, "You owe *<amount of purchase>*. Will that be cash or credit card? We don't accept personal checks or barter." Then the customer should be quickly shooed out of the store and, hopefully, if the service is bad enough, never to be seen again.

The Asshole Customer Factor (ACF)

So far, customers have been assumed to all be little angels. They're well behaved and polite and, of course, always humble. The problem is the dysfunctional company, not the customer. The customer must be riled up because of how they're being treated.

This isn't always the case. There are customers who are pre-irritated before they ask for service or come in the store. These are known as **Pre-Irritated Customers** (**PIC**, pronounced "pick," like icepick or toothpick). They may have just had a bad experience with another dysfunctional company that day, or it could just be a painful hemorrhoid flaring up again.

Some customers just plainly feel they're entitled or the world revolves around them. They don't care if there is a line of people waiting while they ask an inane question unrelated to the product, or want to bore the rep with tales about their expedition to the North Pole.

Sometimes it's hard to tell if the customer is agitated from poor customer service, or is a PIC. The cautious Customer Disservice rep should take precautions, just in case. One way the rep can keep tabs is to calculate the **Asshole Customer Factor (ACF)** per workday, as follows:

$$ACF =$$
$$[(Assholes\ disserved\ in\ a\ day)/$$
$$(Total\ customers\ disserved\ in\ a\ day)] \times 100$$

In these situations, customer avoidance and disservice, is meant to protect the dysfunctional company's employees from bodily harm.

Customers who are particularly obnoxious should be photographed – without their knowledge or consent, of course – and their pictures posted in the office or on the company internal web site. Ideally, the pictures should be posted below the banner, saying "The Customer is the Enemy" with the caption, "If you encounter this customer, they should be treated worse than usual."

This will guarantee even the wimpiest of employees, like those without black belts in a martial art, can defend themselves against nasty intruders.

The Importance of Poor Marketing

Poor marketing is fundamental to the success of the dysfunctional company and works in tandem with Customer Disservice. Products should never work, and services not delivered, as advertised. Marketing is a multi-front war in the dysfunctional company. The battle fields could be advertisements in traditional media, online and through search engines, or social media.

The dysfunctional company fears word-of-mouth marketing. It would show how screwed up the company and its products and services really are. At least with social media, the company can block angry followers or post bogus positive reviews. Word-of-mouth, by definition, is out in the wild, and can't be controlled by the dysfunctional company, and the dysfunctional company doesn't like anything it can't control, especially with its poor and confused messaging.

Marketing communication to customers should be as chaotic and disjointed as its internal communications to its employees. The garbage peddled externally by marketing is just the flip side of the garbage peddled internally. The dysfunctional company chases the latest fad, flipping and flopping from one hot trend to the next, rather than focus on the product's features and strengths, if it even has any, which is always questionable.

It's the job of marketing to dress up the dysfunctional company in nice clothes. Except the clothes never quite fit. The dysfunctional company is constantly changing course. Today the shirt or blouse might fit. Tomorrow it might be too tight or too loose. It's never on target. It either misrepresents the product or service or oversells it, promising the moon and the stars and instead delivering trash from the alley.

The dysfunctional company has no coherent plan for marketing the product or service. Just as it has no overall strategy, as was seen in Habit One, it also has no marketing strategy. Just as it mistakes flash and glamor for real strategy, it uses bling and shiny objects to distract customers from problems with the real product or service.

Yesterday, it showed happy customers frolicking on a beach or in some exotic tropical local. Today, it shows smiling people in an office (definitely not employees imprisoned at the dysfunctional company) or good-looking people walking down a street.

Tomorrow, it shows excited customers in space suits in outer space, smiling through gleaming visors. These people couldn't have been customers of the dysfunctional company. Customers of the dysfunctional company couldn't be that happy, or smiling either. They had to be actors paid lots of money to pretend the product or service works.

Only Smiling Customers, Please

Advertising should only show smiling customers using the product or service. The background should be shiny offices, homes with nicely trimmed lawns or sunny outdoor locations. It should never show real customers frantically trying to get the product to work or waiting for service people who don't show up. It should never show the typical angry and frustrated customer. It should never show customers yelling into their phones, or banging on their laptop keyboards, desperately trying to reach Customer Disservice.

It should never show unhappy customers. It should never show a courtroom where the dysfunctional company is being sued for product defects, or because it injured, maimed or killed a customer, or because the service was incompetent, or poorly delivered, if even delivered, at all. The incessant damage control would overwhelm an army of dysfunctional marketers. It would distract from their daily duty to lie to customers. Marketing at the dysfunctional company is on a mission to deceive.

The dysfunctional company is a master at removing popular features and services at will without informing customers. The product or service should be customized to meet the needs of the company, not the customer. If it's cheaper for the company to remove a feature or drop a service, the feature should be removed or the service dropped.

When a popular feature is removed without notice, customer complaints afterward should be ignored. A popular store in a mall should be closed, for example, because the mall owners want the space for a more expensive store. It doesn't matter if it's unaffordable to customers in the neighborhood, or sells a product of no interest to the locals. On paper it makes more money.

A popular service to a city should be removed, just because it doesn't fit in the schedule. Likewise, the dysfunctional company should stop offering a product or service in popular cities or stores because it's inconvenient for the company to offer. Company convenience always takes precedence over customer convenience. If it works for the company, but not the customer, do it.

Transportation services for both people and goods should be overbooked and overpriced. When the transportation is available, which isn't always the case with the dysfunctional company, it should be regularly delayed and frequently cancelled.

The motto of the dysfunctional transportation company: "We won't get there, so you won't either."

Remember Habit One? If it makes sense, don't do it. These are just more examples. This habit is the dysfunctional gift that keeps on giving.

The dysfunctional company keeps stripping down its products and services, while quietly jacking up the price, hoping customers won't notice.

The dysfunctional company mantra: "Pay more, get less."

This drops the hot potato in the lap of the con artists in marketing to figure out how to spin the latest reduction in the product or service, or justify the newest price increase. If it's new, it must be better, right? Of course, it is to the brain surgeons in dysfunctional marketing. Marketing says last year's model was crap. Buy this year's model? It's better. They never say the real secret. Both last year's and this year's version are still garbage. Any improvements are cosmetic.

Back at the dysfunctional ranch, the marketing cowboys are working on a new campaign to lasso customers.

The Law of Marketing Distraction

Marketing at the dysfunctional company relies on The Law of Marketing Distraction to deceive customers and create brand confusion. The Law of Marketing Distraction confuses the customer by ignoring the product in advertising or marketing promotions in whatever format: broadcast, online or in print. It references everything other than the product to trap customers into buying.

The Law of Marketing Distraction uses two tools: humor and sexual innuendo.

Humor uses a funny story or scene that has nothing to do with the product. In fact, the product or service shouldn't be even mentioned until the end of any advertisement or promotion. The customer is laughing so hard, they forgot about the product and buy it anyways. Funny stories and jokes are more fun than talking about the product.

Of course, the customer won't be laughing after they actually purchase the product. They may soon be crying instead.

Sex always sells, so they say. In the sexual innuendo approach, the marketing material shows a hot babe in a tiny bikini with a hunky guy with six-pack abs in a skimpy swimsuit, both laughing and running hand-in-hand to a backdrop of smooth sand and shimmering seas under a blazing sun and a cloudless sky. As with humor, the product or service shouldn't be disclosed until the end of an advertisement. By this time, the customer is so worked up, they just buy the product, subconsciously thinking it might lead to a mind-blowing sexual experience, even if they weren't looking for sex.

Besides, the product is never used at the beach and should, in fact, not even be used near water. But that doesn't matter. If it sells the product, the dysfunctional company should still market it inappropriately. There is no shame.

Pricing Should be Like Rubber

Once the customer is in the door, or on the phone, it's important to hook them and then reel them in, just like a fish. The best approach is so-called "flexible" pricing. This should give the customer the impression they're getting a good deal when, in fact, they're being screwed up the wazoo.

Pricing should be negotiable – never clearly marked – like in a medieval market, in line with the medieval thinking and practices at the dysfunctional company. The price for one customer for the same product or service should be wildly different than that for the next customer. The name of the game is "Soak the Customer." If one customer actually gets a real discount, the next customer should be overcharged to make up the difference.

The price of anything claiming to be a "good deal" should be so inflated the dysfunctional company is still making out like a bandit even after a steep discount. Sales reps should play head games with customers.

"Let me ring this up separately," the rep might say. "I don't want my manager to know how much they I the price. "We're almost giving it away. We're not making any money." Yeah, right.

Customer Incentive Programs: Not Rewarding

Rewards programs and "customer clubs," particularly if they involve accumulating points for purchases, should be incomprehensible. Points should be difficult, if not impossible, to redeem. There should be tons of rules in fine print with lots of exceptions, black-out dates, and ineligible company or store locations.

Services allowed under reward programs should be restricted to the least amount the dysfunctional company will provide. This isn't saying much, since the dysfunctional company is already providing the worst level of service it can get away with – even on good days.

If the rewards are in the form of discount coupons, they should expire as soon as possible, before the customer even gets a chance to use them. As with rewards points, there should be fine print that can only be read under a microscope, with strict limits on when and where they can be used.

The real purpose of rewards programs and coupons is to fool customers into thinking they're getting a good deal or, heaven forbid, a real discount. The dysfunctional company, of course, would never do this. Real discounts would interfere with their greed. The whiz kids in finance and accounting have already structured these programs to make sure the dysfunctional company, not the customer, comes out ahead.

. . . But Marketing Needs to Hunt Customers Down

While Customer Disservice tries to avoid customers, marketing mercilessly hunts them down with electronic attack dogs like the e-mail blitz and obnoxious ads popping up out of nowhere on social media.

Customers should be constantly bombarded with marketing e-mails, bordering on spam, even for products and services of no interest to them. Links to unsubscribe to the e-mails should be hard to find and then too tiny to read. They shouldn't even use the word "unsubscribe," since that would be too obvious and make it too easy for the customer to escape. Scatter shot marketing is more effective than targeting the right customer.

Inboxes of customers should be as jammed with junk e-mail from the dysfunctional company as are the inboxes of its employees with internal e-mail. This is another example of how chaos inside the company spills over outside the company. In the dysfunctional world, customers should feel the same pain as employees.

The marketing philosophy at the dysfunctional company is "too much is not enough." Just throw everything at the customer, whether they want it or not, and something will eventually stick. If excessive e-mail doesn't do it, then send them text messages, and if that doesn't work, junk mail is always the answer. Keep after them through every possible channel, until they give in.

One clever technique for online customers is the annoying online pop up. Just as the eager customer is about to hit Submit on their shopping cart, a pop-up window should appear with more stuff to throw in at the last minute.

Technology is also key in creating new ways to reach customers, even when they want to be left alone. Intrusion is one of the black arts of marketing at the dysfunctional company. This is just another example of technology as a weapon in the war against customers.

The dysfunctional company wants nothing more than to intrude on the personal lives of customers, gathering as much information as possible from web sites and online services. The proliferation of hi-tech ways to bother customers is insidious. From phone apps that track every customer's movement and activity to surveillance spyware in web sites, the customer is just a nobody standing naked on a street corner waiting to be picked clean by the dysfunctional company.

The dysfunctional company doesn't want to talk to its customers. In fact, the dysfunctional company doesn't want to have anything to do with its customers. The dysfunctional company only wants to invade their privacy for so-called marketing purposes, resell their personal information for a quick buck and, well, of course, take their money.

It's all about misinforming the customer, whether through bad marketing or poor customer services. It's all about squeezing the last dollar out of the customer. This is what the dysfunctional company does best.

The cardinal rule of the dysfunctional company is always: Screw the customer!

The other enemy of the dysfunctional company, its employees, is covered next.

Habit Six:
Drive Out the Best Employees,
Ignore the Rest

"Convicted of embezzlement?
She's perfect for accounting.
She can skip annual ethics training."

Drive Out the Best Employees,
Ignore the Rest

*"I don't know why they aren't accepting our offers.
I only said psychiatric counseling and burial
insurance was included in our health package."*

Employees are a nuisance.

Again, it can't be overemphasized, the twin
enemies of the dysfunctional company are
customers and, of course, employees. Customers
were covered in the last habit, so attention can
now be turned to the other nuisance, employees.

They expect to be paid for their work, and then ask
questions and seek guidance from management.
That's a lot of nerve. On top of that, they expect
annual pay raises and benefits like health insurance
or days off. The line must be drawn somewhere.

If the dysfunctional company could do away with
its employees – replace them with AI-generated
machines or robots – it would. Machines and
robots don't ask questions. They don't ask for
raises either. They also don't go to the bathroom
or take sick days. Hi-tech devices posing as
artificial employees don't disrupt meetings with
lunch or bio breaks.

Customers, at least, are outside the company, out of sight and out of mind. They can be forgotten altogether. Employees, on the other hand can't be ignored. They're a nagging tooth ache inside the body of the company.

Employees are told to "think outside the box" and then their ideas are discarded, criticized or somehow forgotten, added to a long list of lost to-do items in a hidden file on an anonymous laptop in management. Employees are told to send suggestions to an anonymous e-mail box, which, like the employees themselves, is ignored and then deleted.

The dysfunctional company talks about employee "engagement and empowerment," and then neither engages nor empowers any employees. Management nods its agreement when face-to-face with employees but then tosses their ideas aside behind their back. The Cabal of Insiders can never relinquish power to its employees.

The dysfunctional company hates its employee's families. Families get in the way of keeping the employee chained to their work, or non-work. The dysfunctional company demands complete loyalty and gives little or nothing in return.

Employees should never have to deal with illness, kids, or sick or elderly family, or births and deaths. The dysfunctional company never gives priority to any life or family events. The kid has a once-in-a-lifetime championship game. Not on our time. These aren't excuses for missing work.

The dysfunctional company has no boundaries with employees. It schedules meetings and sends e-mails even during vacation, or a "day off." Day off? There is no such thing. Time off doesn't exist at the dysfunctional company. Everybody is expected to be connected, and available, at all times, 24x7, even on "holidays," company or otherwise.

The dysfunctional company treats employees like line items in the budget that can be removed at any time. Nobody is really safe at the dysfunctional company. The Grim Reaper could strike at any moment. A reorganization here, a management change there, arbitrary reassignment to a new group for no reason, redundancy through a merger or acquisition, it could happen suddenly without warning. It could all happen with just a click of a mouse in HR.

People in purchasing could be transferred to sanitation, marketing folks could end up in IT, or salespeople could move to engineering or R&D. So-called "exciting new opportunities," or "new frontiers" are endless. Job placement at the dysfunctional company is like a game of musical chairs, someone eventually loses their seat. The hapless employee never knows where he or she will end up. It's part of the adventure of the work journey, like a safari through the company wilderness without pith helmets to catch flying bullshit or machetes to cut through the thicket.

Creative people with great ideas need not apply. The best employees should be driven from the organization, hounded out and micromanaged. A good employee can never be trusted. Those with energy and enthusiasm will eventually get exhausted from non-stop bureaucratic battles and office politics and endless crippling procedures and rules. They're innovators who will try to improve the product or service, maybe even streamline processes. This is totally unacceptable.

In the dysfunctional company, the cream doesn't rise to the top. It sinks to the bottom and is flushed out. Political muscle and raw power and, of course, internal connections, not talent or skill, are what counts.

Eventually, like someone who eats poorly, the cholesterol will build up in the company veins. Then comes the heart attack, and it stops functioning or, at least, ceases to function as a business. It will be just another non-functional bureaucratic mess staffed by mediocre yes-people.

The visionary founder of the company is long gone. He or she couldn't even get a job at their own company today. They would be laughed out of the organization, considered too intelligent, too radical, too competent. They wouldn't even know how to properly fill out the endless paperwork to get anything done.

The dysfunctional company still needs to hire people to keep limping along. It still needs to appear functional to the outside world. It still needs to follow the Principle of the Appearance of Activity.

It all starts with the hiring process.

The Job Requisition:
The Start of the Descent into Hiring Hell

The first step is for an executive or manager to decide they need to create a position, or fill an existing position abandoned by an employee carted off in a straitjacket (a real one, not the bureaucratic kind) to a mental hospital.

The dysfunctional company never gets its hiring needs right. Its cumbersome bureaucracy has no idea how many people it really needs. After waves of layoffs, poor forecasting based on voodoo metrics, it has lost track of its own people. It hires either too many people, or too few.

When there aren't enough employees – as usually happens after waves of layoffs – the remaining employees are overworked and under water. When it hires too many, there isn't enough work to go around. Then, again, in the dysfunctional company, it's never clear who is really doing productive work and who is just doing bureaucratic support nonsense – or maybe doing a good job of loafing around while looking busy – The Principle of the Appearance of Activity. This adds to the difficulties in calculating hiring needs.

Then there is the situation where the existing team actually is adequate. They only appear to need help since they're too distracted to do productive work – remember Productive Work from Habit One? If the team were given a bureaucratic laxative, they could expel some of their crap – unnecessary rules and procedures, bureaucratic cat fights, forced socializing, excessive meetings and e-mails – and actually get to work.

The out-of-touch hiring managers and executives, who have no idea what their group or department is up to anyways, still just goes ahead and creates a job requirement and requisition.

The position now anointed from on high, the next step is to get the wheels of HR spinning to fill the opening with the wrong candidate. As will be seen, the best candidates are invisible to the automated hi-tech processes of the dysfunctional HR department.

Non-Hiring Practices Guaranteed to Miss Talent

Just like Customer Disservice, the recruiting department of HR should be barred from direct contact with the public. The system should be entirely automated to guarantee quality candidates are never found.

Even if a candidate finds a suitable job on the company web site, or through an advertisement or social media posting, the process to get hired should be unclear and complex. The would-be hire will get a taste for the rigorous bureaucratic hoops they will face on the job. The byzantine hiring process will prepare the candidate for daily life at the dysfunctional company.

Job descriptions need to be equally vague and confusing. Skills irrelevant to the job should be included. For example, for accounting positions, the ability to sing and dance may be required for presenting weak financials to executives. Company training recruits should know how to fold paper airplanes for sending out schedules of new classes around the office. Customer Disservice reps should know how to play the harmonica to kill time during long hold times on the phone with angry customers.

IT people should have people skills and be able to sell. IT people should be required to have knowledge of every known computer skill, even those not used anymore, going back to the abacus and Roman numerals. If a programming language, or network or hardware device, is obsolete, it should be listed in the long laundry list of the job requisition. Each IT candidate will be thoroughly questioned, and expected to demonstrate during the interview competence in unnecessary and outdated tech skills.

And all candidates should be expected to know how to clean toilets, cook and clean in the company cafeteria, or lift heavy boxes and drive forklifts or trucks. You never know when these skills might come in handy in the office, or if the candidate will suddenly be reassigned mysteriously to warehouse and maintenance duties.

The Online Job Site:
Sinkholes for Resumes

The process starts with the candidate submitting a resume through the company web site. The candidate will then be notified by a cryptic e-mail their resume has been received. Poorly worded e-mails are preferred to just simply saying, "Your resume has been received." Again, this is preparation for what lies ahead if the inattentive candidate gets hired.

Then the trail goes cold.

The candidate never hears from the company again. In fact, nobody at the dysfunctional company ever sees the resume. It goes to an automated system that scans the resume for keywords. Only a fraction of resumes ever reaches a human. This ensures that an outstanding candidate who has a creative resume, or uses creative language that might just fit the bill, will never get in the door.

It's also possible, just like the anonymous e-mailbox for suggestions from employees, the resume goes into an e-garbage can, never to be seen again. It's also possible the job doesn't exist. It could be just a phantom posting. Dysfunctional companies are known for building up reserves of resumes they never use. It couldn't possibly be for future recruits. That would make sense.

A good workaround is for the candidate to simply put the word "asshole" at random somewhere in the middle of the resume. The dysfunctional company's resume scanners should pick this up immediately – though, as with everything else at the dysfunctional company, there is no guarantee – and flag the resume for review. If nothing else, the resume will be added to the company's Asshole Reserve Army (ARA) database to suddenly replace someone who may have recently perished during an unfortunate bureaucratic incident.

Sure, large companies that are inundated with massive numbers of resumes need a screening process. The dysfunctional company, however, always finds ways to mess up even no-brainer automated processes with bureaucratic bottlenecks. There are surprise extra approvals and then stupid requests like "We need additional documentation to proceed with your application." Who knew a DNA test was required for applying to this company? Communication is all done, in the spirit of the dysfunctional company, through anonymous e-mails, to avoid actual contact with the candidate.

After not hearing from the company, the candidate may apply again, thinking their original submission was lost – very likely at the dysfunctional company.

The frustrated job-seeker may then try to send e-mails or, perish the thought, try to call the dysfunctional company for a status on their application.

Quality candidates will, at some point, just move on and apply to other companies. This leaves only the desperate, the confused and the lonely – or just the insane – to continue banging their head on the door of the dysfunctional company, making sure only mediocre employees apply and get hired. The dysfunctional company is a halfway house for people who can't get jobs anywhere else.

The Byzantine Interview Process

In the million-to-one chance the candidate gets called for an interview, the dysfunctional company can't show its true colors to prospective employees. If the interview is done by video conference, a beach background gives the impression this is a fun place to work. Little does the candidate know.

If the interview is in-person at the company office, HR will have to do some scrambling. The candidate must always be accompanied by someone from HR. No exceptions.

The recruit should be escorted into a windowless private room, away from any cubicle farms or workspace benches and definitely far from the screaming and moaning in the Free Fire Zones, which will be introduced shortly.

If touring the office at any time before or after the interview, the candidate should never be allowed to see employees in open combat, yelling at each other or fist fighting and any conference rooms with auditors should be avoided. HR should only route the candidate through areas where employees are happy and smiling, even if they've been drugged up for the occasion to give a good impression.

If the candidate has to go to the bathroom, again, they need to be accompanied by HR. The bathroom needs to be cleared of vomit bags ahead of time by maintenance. Employees about to throw up, or who have passed out, should also be removed. Bathrooms need to be pristine and odor free and, of course, fully functional with flushing toilets – working and not backed up – and running water.

The candidate may ask uncomfortable questions. HR should be prepared. They may have heard the company has a reputation for high rates of mental illness and premature deaths. The candidate should be assured that psychiatric services and life and burial insurance are included in the company health care plan. This should calm the nerves of even the most squeamish potential future employees.

The candidate should always be asked, "Why do you want to work here? (Implied: "No sane person does. Only a masochist would work here.)"

The following are acceptable answers:
"I don't know."
"Someone in a bar told me this would be a shitty place to work."
"I believe in redemption through suffering."
"I heard this company builds character. It was either this or the military, and I'm a coward."

HR may also hear sob stories from candidates unhappy at their current dysfunctional company.

A perfect candidate might say something like:
"I can't get anything done at my company. I'm looking for a new opportunity, where I can make an impact."

As soon as the HR rep, and hiring manager hears the wonderful words, "new opportunity" or "make an impact," signal flares should go up. These are the magic buzzwords every potential hire should say.

Immediately, HR will think they have a live one, and may want to short circuit the hiring process, bypassing the lie detector tests and the mandatory waterboarding session. They know this is someone they can mold in the company image and eventually beat down into a pulp once hired.

New Hires:
Value Added or Damage Control?

The interview process should proceed next with personal questions totally unrelated to the job posting. The secret agenda of the dysfunctional company is to ascertain the candidate's character through pointed and specific questions. Vagueness isn't appropriate here.

The idea isn't to find out what value the candidate might add to the dysfunctional company, but how much damage they might cause the dysfunctional company, and if that damage can be contained. Damage control is key. Valued added is secondary.

The next round of interviews might start with a question like, "What is your greatest weakness?" This type of question is just too lame. A better, more direct, question should be, "What was your biggest screw up at your last company? Did you resolve it? If you didn't resolve it, how did you cover it up?"

This cuts to the heart of the matter, and helps the interviewer determine if the candidate might cause damage to the dysfunctional company, or if the candidate can successfully hide his or her transgressions.

If the employee can be trusted to hide important mistakes from management, they can be counted on to deceive the public, when the ship capsizes. This is an important consideration for all new recruits.

Here is a sample of questions for effectively assessing character:

1. If you could have a pet, would it be a dog, a cat or a snake?
2. Who is your favorite brutal dictator, living or dead?
3. Who would you want to be stranded with on a deserted island?

The best candidates are those who answer with the deadliest animal, the most brutal dictator, and the kinkiest person to be stranded with. If the candidate gets emotional and choked up, when talking about their favorite dictator, this is a good sign. Another plus is if a photo of the dictator is the screen saver on their cell phone. Screen savers with kids or family or pets are signs of weakness and show too much humanity for the dysfunctional company.

The dysfunctional company sees employees as a necessary evil, warm bodies only to be hired as a last resort to attempt to get work done. The dysfunctional company isn't interested in the positive the candidate brings to the table, but whether the table is knocked over, and if it can be fixed. Again, damage control over value added.

The contribution of the potential new employee is less important than their downside risk to the company.

The dysfunctional company sees each recruit not as an asset, but as a potential liability to be controlled or throttled, if need be. Each new employee is not welcomed as a new member of the team, but as a threat to be treated with suspicion. The new employee is guilty until proven innocent and is only fully accepted after completely assimilating the company's dark and arcane culture.

The sticky subject of salary will inevitably come up next during interviews, despite HR's best efforts to avoid the subject. Salaries at the dysfunctional company are often a bizarre mix totally unrelated to the market for the specific position. Two employees doing the same job in the same department, maybe even sitting next to each other, may have wildly different salaries. One may be working at minimum wage, and the other making six figures.

In any case, salary negotiations, like everything else at the dysfunctional company, should be contentious and drawn out until the candidate finally gives up and accepts the lowest possible salary.

Candidates should be ranked by the recruiter after the interview by color codes – green (a real sleaze ball piece of trash, who would be essential to the company), yellow (borderline psychopaths) and red (no way, too high quality).

Extending the Offer and Subsequent Background Checks

Once the interviews and salary negotiations have been completed, the candidate may be extended a written offer.

The vetting process now begins.

A background check may uncover some interesting things. Positive drug tests, if required, should be ignored as long as the employee as sober in the office. Pesky little convictions for various felonies should also be overlooked, especially if the candidate has skills valuable to the dysfunctional company.

Candidates for sales should be screened to make sure they're pathological liars. They should be able to show they can use high-pressure sales techniques to strong arm customers. Potential salespeople also need to be aware transparent pricing is not a dysfunctional company strength.

During interviews, candidates need to demonstrate proficiency in the following pricing tactics: bait-and-switch, last minute surcharges and hidden fees in the fine print in contracts. Another real plus is if they can show they have hooked customers into signing multi-year contracts, which supposedly can be cancelled, but only with astronomic "termination" fees.

Candidates for finance, bookkeeping and accounting should likewise come from shady backgrounds. They should have worked for companies on the verge of – or have contributed to their – financial collapse and be adept at manipulating numbers. Those with prior criminal records for white collar crimes, especially for fraud and embezzlement, should be encouraged to apply. The less ethical, the better.

Prior convictions for fraud are also good indicators for candidates for marketing. This shows they won't be afraid to make false claims, or misrepresent, the product or service to the public. If they can con HR into hiring them, they con anyone, especially customers.

Criminal records for theft should be overlooked for candidates for purchasing. Candidates for auditors, likewise, with histories of mental illness involving sadism or torture should be on the top of the resume pile.

Lawyers being considered for the legal department should have no morals or ethics. They should be bulldogs prepared to do whatever dirty work the company needs in its war against customers.

Background checks for legal department candidates should uncover brushes with their local bar association, evidence they're not afraid to push the envelope. As long as they haven't been disbarred and are still members in good standing, they're eligible candidates. It wouldn't be appropriate even for the dysfunctional company to stoop so low as to hire a defrocked attorney.

Candidates for legal should also have an attitude. Arrogance is a positive trait. Sissies aren't welcome. The legal department in many dysfunctional companies has some of the highest ADRs, often even higher than the ADR of the Lords of IT, also known for being staffed with attitude.

For all candidates, DUI and drug convictions are a plus since they show the candidate can function in the altered state of awareness required to get any work done at the dysfunctional company.

Honesty isn't a virtue in the dysfunctional company. It's definitely a liability and candidates displaying honesty and integrity should be screened out immediately during the hiring process.

Honesty is never the best policy. Honesty could solve a problem. Honesty could mean admitting a mistake. Honesty could lead to open communication. This can't be tolerated. It would make sense.

Lies, lies and more lies, and covering up should be the rule of the day for every individual at all levels. It's all about self-preservation in the dysfunctional company. The well-being of co-workers just doesn't count.

Honesty could lead to cooperation and to that other anathema of the dysfunctional company: teamwork.

In the dysfunctional company, teamwork is nonsense. It's everybody for themselves. If somebody needs to be tossed off the life boat, so be it. Any candidate who says they're a "team player" during the interview, or who shows signs of teamwork, needs to be filtered out. This type of activity needs to be nipped in the bud to prevent the "teamwork" virus from infecting the company.

HR should also play careful attention to possible independent and free thinkers. These people need to be weeded out from the resume pool immediately. Intelligence and personality tests should carry more weight than face-to-face interviews. Personality tests should label the candidate with a nifty string of letters, only a psychologist could interpret. For example, the ideal candidate should be an "**IHAP**," meaning "I Have Asshole Potential," to use psychobabble terminology.

Resumes where the candidate claims to be "results oriented" should be thrown out immediately. This is a vague term, hinting the recruit might attempt to do real work at the company. It's never really clear what "results" the candidate had achieved or is trying to achieve. It could be anything from increasing sales to a clever marketing plan that crashed and burned, or maybe an innovation to the product or service that failed upon launch.

Instead of minimum IQs, there should be an IQ ceiling, over which candidates need not apply. Serial failures and screw ups from prior dysfunctional companies are the ideal candidate.

It's a gray area whether to hire job hoppers. On the one hand, their defects are a plus for the dysfunctional company. On the other hand, they might not hang around long enough to cause sufficient damage.

Everything should be documented clearly in their resumes, which should be crisp and clear but full of typos and inflated information. Fluff is an important part of the ideal dysfunctional resume. What the candidate claims on their resume shouldn't match what appears in the background check. Jobs listed should be unable to be verified.

For example, a candidate's resume might list "hospitality specialist" on their resume. The hotel mentioned as the place of employment might not exist. The applicant is probably covering up her prior employment as a madame at a local brothel. That makes here a good fit for the dysfunctional company – shady yet customer-oriented. She would know how to handle the company's frequent sticky situations with customers.

Educational degrees claimed should be bogus. This kind of outright lying shouldn't be a problem – a real asset for prospective sales people – especially if the candidate came from other dysfunctional companies, whose HR departments might have spotty verification procedures.

Dates shouldn't jive with actual time worked, and there should be unexplained gaps in employment, an effective way to cover prison time. If asked about any gaps, the former convict can simply say they took time off to "find themselves," which usually means trying out different job assignments in the prison's work-release program.

New Hire Disorientation and Onboarding

The onboarding process for new employees at the dysfunctional company includes one or more disorientation sessions and then adding them to the HR system. These two steps can be done together or separately, depending on how screwed up the dysfunctional company handles onboarding.

As expected, the dysfunctional company gets the employee on the wrong track from the start with messed up onboarding procedures.

Employees at the dysfunctional company need to be tracked like cattle. They should be tagged and given an ID number before being entered into a company database. Issuing an ID number is the easy part. Even the dysfunctional company can do that. The problem is tagging. Stapling a tag to the employee's ear, as is done with livestock, isn't recommended and might even be illegal in some areas. The preferred method is bar coding.

New employees need to be numbered and bar coded, so they can be tracked throughout the system at any time, whether in the office, or at their remote location. In fact, preferences should be given to candidates coming from other dysfunctional companies where they have already been bar coded.

If the new employee hasn't been bar coded yet, this can be done either during Disorientation, or right after, before the employee is assigned to their PAWS.

The next step before immediately starting work is attending **New Hire Disorientation**. No one is really hired to get any work done. That will become clear quickly during Disorientation, which will get the happy new employee limbered up and in tip top shape for the bureaucratic jousting to follow. Remote employees, who may never set foot in the office again, will still be expected to go to an office to attend Disorientation training in person.

A key part of Disorientation training is getting to know the Lords of IT, who were introduced in Habit Two as one of the many players in the company's never-ending turf battles. They provide the most important weapon for the new hires: their laptops.

The first step in Disorientation is for the Lords of IT to get laptops into the eager hands of the new recruits. Nobody in the company can function – or dysfunction – without their laptop.

This requires the presence of an actual member of royalty from the Lords of IT at the first Disorientation session. This will be the only time employees actually see a breathing – or friendly and smiling – human being from IT in the office. This gives the false impression IT staff are available – and helpful – to come by and help at any time. Nothing is further from the truth, as employees soon find out, during their first outage.

But, then very little during Disorientation gives the recruit an accurate picture of the company.

Laptops now, hopefully, set up, the recruits can start doing the considerable paperwork to get them processed and into the HR and company systems.

They will then hear a series of boring and cookie cutter presentations from various departments around the company, again, giving the false impression these departments run smoothly.

One presentation will be a fairy tale with the history of the company and how its leaders descended from ancient Gods on some faraway mountain top nobody ever heard of and probably doesn't exist. Black and white photos of the founders, with mustaches and button-down vests, from the 1800s, probably bought at random from some antique shop, will be displayed. If the founders are from the Twentieth Century or later, the photos will be of them as teenagers climbing a mountain, or tossing around a utility pole, or doing some other athletic activity.

Displays of athletic prowess by executives are common in dysfunctional companies to foster the myth they're all-powerful creatures with magical abilities. The only magical power they have is screwing up companies.

Next the employees will be given their survival kits, all packed in a cheap duffle bag with the company logo with the following essential items:

- Water bottles
- Vomit bags
- Bandages and ointment
- Laser pointers
- List of phone numbers and e-mails for assistance

A bag or duffle bag with the company logo should be standard issue to all employees at every dysfunctional event, not just at Disorientation. Employees should have closets full of bags, more than they would ever need. If a duffle bag isn't provided, it isn't an authentic company event. And if it has some other dysfunctional company's logo, someone in purchasing screwed up again.

Water bottles with the company logo are also standard issue for use in both the PAWs and meetings. Employees must keep hydrated during long hours in meetings to stay alert and fresh. As with duffle bags, these are handed out at every event, small or large, or sometimes they just show up at random for no reason at the PAWS.

Also, as with duffle bags, employees end up with more water bottles than they could ever use in their lifetime or the lifetimes of several generations of their offspring. Some clever employees have been known to stack them up in pyramids at their PAWS, during multitasking, and use them for storage of bits of paper, office supplies or snacks and extra vomit bags.

After the duffle bag and the water bottle, the survival kit should include a starter set of vomit bags with the company logo. This will be for the frequent bouts of nausea they will experience each day. Road warriors will be expected to collect vomit bags from the airlines they use when traveling. Other office-bound and remote employees, unfortunately, will have to go through the hassle of dealing with purchasing to replenish their supply of vomit bags.

Bandages and antiseptic ointment are included for when employees bang their heads against the wall. These won't be sufficient for the many times when employees will want to slash their wrists, sometimes during meetings.   In these situations, an ambulance should be called. The company dispensary, if there is one, won't be able to handle the profuse bleeding.

Then there are laser pointers for use during meetings, as has already been discussed in Habit Four. Employees can use these either to disrupt or participate in the meeting. This helps the employee feel they're making a contribution, which management usually ignores.

Finally, there is a list of phone numbers and e-mails for assistance. There are contacts for IT, mental health, HR and, amazingly, even an ethics hotline to report wrong doing and abuses. Most of the numbers and e-mails have been disconnected and the contact names are for people long gone from the company. Internal assistance to employees should mirror the poor service customers get when daring to contact the company, as was seen in Habit Five. This will give the employee a taste of what their customers endure, trying to get help from the company.

After disorientation, the next step in onboarding is giving the employee a place to work. Security guards should be waiting to escort the Disorientation graduate in handcuffs to their new PAWS.

The Importance of Company Branded Swag

Once situated, each employee should decorate their PAWS with company paraphernalia. These include pens, notepads, sticky notes, of course, and mugs, all with the company logo. Then there are staplers, cheap little plastic clocks, wall calendars, desk calendars, and even fake gold plaques with inspirational sayings like "How did I screw the customer today?" The best are little rubber stress balls with the company logo. Unfortunately, as is expected at the dysfunctional company, these wear out quickly from frequent use.

Letter openers with the dysfunctional company logo are another great idea. Any other sharp objects, like spindles, and small office knives and box cutters, should be avoided to prevent mishaps between tense employees. While it's important to keep tensions high in the office, employees shouldn't be killing each other. Then HR has to back fill positions, which is always a problem, since it engages the unwieldy bureaucratic machinery again.

Then there is company clothing. The possibilities are endless for spreading the company logo: t-shirts, caps, ties and even underwear and socks. Since underwear isn't normally visible, except in the company bathrooms, it doesn't make sense to have unseen logos. This is the dysfunctional company, so it's a good idea.

However, as was discussed in Habit Four, if the company has a CUP, company-branded underwear may be required for all meeting attendees.

Ideally, employees should always be wearing company clothing while at their PAWS to complement the company swag on their desk. This is a sign of company loyalty and may help mitigate penalties when auditors come by to make an arrest.

Another clever idea in the unseen logo category is a condom with the company logo. Under HR rules, these can't be used in the office, only at approved forced socialization events. As with everything else at the dysfunctional company, company condom use is monitored and subject to audit review and findings.

The rule of only wearing clothing with company logos also applies to remote employees, whose compliance is monitored via the surveillance software on their laptop. The software should filter out kids or angry pets in the background, screaming or yelping at weird or poorly designed logos on clothing and duffle bags, scattered around the house.

The employee settled in at their PAWS can finally start, or attempt to start, their workday.

The Dysfunctional Daily Routine

For the employee at the dysfunctional company, the workday is full of challenges. There are countless obstacles to overcome just to get to first base. Getting anything done is really iffy.

The two most important rituals first thing in the morning are desk calisthenics and starting the laptop followed by checking the org chart for a pulse.

The employee may first want to do some simple calisthenics at her PAWS to prepare for the stressful day ahead. These might include stretching exercises – head rolls to loosen up the neck to prevent whiplash, and arm and leg stretches to prevent cramps during long hours sitting in meetings or at her PAWS. Office athletes have been known to pull their hamstrings when running from auditors in hot pursuit. Stretching first thing in the morning gets the employee limbered up to prevent these injuries.

The employee next then turns on her laptop. This is the scariest part of the day. If the laptop doesn't boot up, no work, not even pointless bureaucratic nonsense, can be done. The dysfunctional company laptop has been loaded up with all kinds of garbage – surveillance software, standard issue company software – some of which can take several minutes, if not half a day, or days, to load up.

Mysterious windows open and close, icons spin around like tops and little images on the desktop flash and disappear in the blink of an eye. If there is a system update or security patch, the process could take longer. Even on good days, booting up can take forever.

The well-prepared employee prays to the Lords of IT before booting up in the morning. This is just part of every employee's morning rituals. It's a good idea to have a mug – with the company logo, or course – sitting in the PAWS for putting offerings to the Lords of IT. Some suggested offerings are crumpled up pieces of old paycheck stubs, bits of dirt from the parking lot, twigs, pennies, or dandelions. A dead mouse from the company cafeteria is always effective.

It's a good sign when the screen finally displays the company logo, spinning like a top, or in orbit around a planet. This means the system might boot up. She keeps her fingers crossed.

Today, the system booted up, and the employee logs in. Today, she was lucky. She was able to logon to her system. In the dysfunctional company, even logging in is an ordeal involving multiple user IDs and passwords. Security should be so tight it keeps employees out, but allows hackers to get in.

The clock is ticking. A half hour has already passed. She still hasn't accomplished anything.

IT Systems Should Be Down During the Workday

What about those days when the system doesn't boot up, or she can't log in? Then she has to call the Lord of IT's Helpless Desk, another whole bureaucratic adventure in itself, as has already been seen.

IT should never announce when system updates are scheduled. That would make sense and is, therefore, unacceptable. Instead, employees should be kept on their toes, not knowing when to plan work around planned system outages. Maintenance windows should be a secret. They should be scheduled for the busiest part of the day, like first thing in the morning, rather than when systems aren't being used much, such as overnight or on weekends. Again, that would make sense, under Habit One, and can't be allowed.

All upgrades should make sure systems are more complicated, more difficult to worse, more confusing, and less user-friendly. They should be an open invitation to clog up the Helpless Desk with more calls than usual from frantic employees. This is a typical day at the dysfunctional company, just another unplanned roadblock in an already screwed up day.

IT systems should go down at critical moments. A nice touch is when the system goes down for an unexpected installation of an emergency patch right in the middle of an important presentation by the CEO to the entire company. The screen going blank in the middle of a presentation inspires confidence in employees. If the CEO is announcing a mass layoff, employees would have no idea why they're being suddenly escorted out of the building. They might think it's just a fire drill, instead of another mass execution in the parking lot. This just adds to the normal confusion and miscommunication the Cabal of Insiders creates every day.

Mandatory Daily Org Chart Checks

Assuming the employee is still employed is another great mystery of the dysfunctional universe. The first thing the employee should do after booting up is look themselves up on the organization chart. With constant unnecessary reorganizations, sudden layoffs and general confusion among management about their exact responsibilities, the employee may have no idea who she reports to, or even if she reports to anyone. She's not sure she's even still an employee. This changes every day, maybe multiple times in a day.

The typical org chart at the dysfunctional company, even on a good day, looks like a spaghetti bowl without marinara or Bolognese. This employee is connected to this or that manager, who might be connected to some vice president on Mars, and then to another executive in another galaxy, maybe even two or three of them simultaneously in so-called "matrix" organizations. In some cases, there might be so many levels above the employee, she needs earth moving equipment to be excavated out of the hole.

She may suddenly notice she isn't on the org chart today. A whole section of the org chart she used to inhabit is now missing. It calved off like an iceberg from a polar glacier during yesterday's mass layoff. She is now officially a **Company Orphan (CO)**. Just as someone in battle may be Missing in Action (MIA), the equivalent in the dysfunctional company is **Missing in Bureaucracy (MIB)**. The CO is MIB – a nice example of a bi-acronym sentence, per Habit Three.

She nervously sends an e-mail to HR, which is already backed up this morning with thousands of e-mails from other MIBs. Miraculously, she finally gets through the same century, and HR confirms that she is still employed and still getting a paycheck.

That hurdle overcome; the employee can now focus on the important part of her day – getting nothing done.

The day of obstacles is finally now ready to begin.

It starts with the endless e-mails in her inbox. Expanding further on the theme of e-mails discussed in Habit Three, there are the perpetual problems endemic to the dysfunctional companies: lost orders, misscheduled or incomplete projects, cost overruns, multiple requests for the same information from different departments, requests and responses for approvals and other bureaucratic games. There are forms to fill out, and more forms again, especially for minor requests, and then reports about the lack of reports.

There is in inverse relationship in the dysfunctional company between the importance of a request and its required paperwork. The smaller the request, the more approvals required. Don't even begin to ask about what's required for a bathroom break.

There are sticky notes plastered all over her monitor telling her about this or that useless activity that has to be done that day. There are sticky notes with passwords for the several systems she has to log into just to get a cup of coffee. There are sticky notes with reminders for every project she is trying, but never able, to either work on or complete, or maybe even get started. There are sticky notes to remind her to use sticky notes or, when her supply is running low, to get more.

Sticky notes help her get through the day. When the sticky notes run out, she can't function. Then the comes the life-and-death decision – "Do I go through purchasing, or just buy them myself down the street?"

Then there are unnecessary but mandatory classes – having nothing to do with the employee's job – requested by this manager, or that executive because they think it's a good idea. Company training has already been covered in detail in Habit Three about poor communication. The following is an example of how training might work to foul up a typical day at the dysfunctional company.

More precious time is wasted. The clock is ticking.

The employee may suddenly get an ominous e-mail, out of nowhere, saying such-and-such class must be taken or it will be noted in the employee's personnel file – maybe in conflict resolution, maybe about some obscure labor law, maybe about cafeteria maintenance and sanitation, maybe about ethics for the dishonest or the corrupt and the ethically challenged, maybe about some new IT system the employee never uses. The e-mail comes from some anonymous bot, to which the employee can't respond. Of course, no human is mentioned where a question can be directed.

E-mail almost cleared away – though it still keeps on coming, even when the employee is asleep or after hours – it's time for a chain of non-stop meetings. Meetings as a dysfunctional tool have already been discussed extensively in Habit Four. As with excessive e-mail, the following are examples of meetings ruining a typical day at the dysfunctional company.

There is the weekly status meeting (remember TWMs from Habit One?) to rehash no progress since the last meeting, and then meetings that were automatically assigned for no reason. There are meetings just to keep the employee in meetings and finally meetings to decide if there should be more meetings.

In industries where annual training is required for Continuing Education (CE) credits, if the employee doesn't meet their CE quota, HR should send them an e-mail notification of a "CE Deficiency." In this case, the employee should get a note from their doctor saying they're taking medication for their CE Deficiency and send it to HR.

Then there are customer complaints to resolve. There are so many screw ups from poor products and services sometimes it seems the whole day is spent just cleaning up one mess after another.

It's now almost noon.

Exhausted from chasing her tail with e-mails and meetings, the employee had hoped to get some work done over lunch. But no, the dysfunctional company even had that planned out. Forced socialization, especially with co-workers she can't stand, is de rigueur. Her manager had scheduled a compulsory ice cream social for the team. She is relieved this doesn't involve the heavy drinking usually required at other forced social activities. This was deliberately planned for the middle of the day to disrupt as much work as possible. If liquor had been involved, unlike today, the rest of the day would have been shot.

She mistakenly thinks she can come back to her PAWS and get down to business: writing that proposal, closing a sale or working on a project to improve service. Suddenly, she notices a group of employees gathering in the conference room across from her desk. They don't look like other employees. They look more serious. They're wearing arm bands and are setting up laptops and opening files on the table. They set up an interrogation flood light and are attaching straps to a chair for restraints. Once settled in, they turn down the lights and close the shades.

The auditors have arrived, and their fangs are out. She knows their roles in this company fairy tale. They're the Fox (Audit), and she is Little Red Riding Hood (Employee). Her day is about to go haywire.

She sees them looking at her out of the corner of her eye. Someone comes over and summons here into the room. They turn on, and then, dim the lights for theatrical effect. As she was taught in disorientation training, under the Geneva Convention for captured employee prisoners of war, she only has to give her name, job title and employee ID.

She knows why they summoned her. It was her expense report. Yes, she knew she blew her marketing budget when she spent tens of thousands of dollars for an army of male and female strippers for a customer function. Yes, she also knew it violated the company's sexual harassment policy. But it was a big client and there was a lot of money at stake, so the Cabal of Insiders let it slide.

She still is traumatized from the last time she was burned at the stake by audit. It was also about her expense report. It was small, but she still has flashbacks from being severely punished. It was about her purchase of one small pad of sticky notes for just a few dollars at a local stationery store.

They strung her up on the rack and forced her to confess. It was painful, but she survived and lived to tell about it.

The employee returns to her PAWS. She sees there is only fifteen minutes left in the workday. The day is almost over. There's only enough time left for a smoking or bathroom break, and even that hasn't been approved by her supervisors.

She tells herself, "Well, there's always tomorrow. Another day to get nothing done." Then she gets a bright idea. There still is time for a good old-fashioned D&R, as mentioned in Habit Three.

The PAWS is only for a single employee. The employee isn't an isolated entity in the dysfunctional universe. He or she is part of a constellation of PAWS that make up the geography of the company.

Office Organization: The Key Role of Row Captains

The importance of PAWS for commanding and controlling employees has been a consistent theme throughout this book. The dysfunctional company uses the PAWS for keeping control over employee whereabouts, since employees can't be trusted to move freely around the office without supervision. They might actually try to do productive work or even have a good idea if they move around. They might even do the unthinkable and try to talk to other employees and contribute to productive work. This has to be stopped.

The next level up from the PAWS is the row.

The office should be divided up into rows along lines of cubicles or workspaces. Each row should have a designated **Row Captain**. The role of the Row Captain is to periodically walk up and down rows of PAWSs and make sure employees are sitting up straight and have their headphones attached properly for mandatory dial-in meetings.

Row Captains can also string barbed wire between sections of the office to make rows feel like combat trenches.

In the unlikely event HR doesn't allow barbed wire to be strung around the office, another key role of Row Captains is to create row fights. Without warning, a Row Captain should stand up on his or her desk and yell at the next row, "My row can beat up your row," or "Your row sucks." This should result in fist fights between rows to keep things perfectly dysfunctional.

For remote employees, one member of their online group can be designated as a remote Row Captain, periodically spying on employees through company-issued web cams installed on their laptops.

Whether office-based or remote, cubicle or workspace dweller should always know who is their Row Captain. The Row Captain's work area in the office should be clearly marked with an "RC" sign to avoid any confusion. For remote employees, the "RC" can be in the upper-right corner of their picture on the icon on the messaging app on their desktop.

Row Captains, as will be seen, are also responsible for dealing with employees who drop dead at their PAWS.

Office Geography: Mixing the Incompatible

The location of departments within the office is a vital part of running the dysfunctional company. Incompatible departments, which wouldn't be expected to get along, should be located next to each other.

For example, marketing should be next to accounting. Marketing people, by their nature, are a lively bunch. They're friendly and outgoing. They sing jingles and wear funny hats, thinking of ways to promote the company's products and services. They're usually laughing as they bounce around ideas for new marketing campaigns. The noise and merriment often spread to neighboring parts of the office.

They have to laugh. Otherwise, they would be crying. They have a tall order, trying to put lipstick on the pig that is the dysfunctional company. It isn't easy selling the shoddy products or services the dysfunctional company is peddling to the public. It takes the most creative minds – "liars" would be too strong a word – to sell garbage.

Accounting people, on the other hand, are stern and quiet. Many are introverted and dour individuals who relate better to numbers than people. They're quiet and diligent, heads down looking at spreadsheets all day. Their task is even more ominous. They have to "make the numbers work" on a sinking ship with erratic sales. While marketing tries to make the company look good to the public, the outside world, so to speak, the mission of accounting is to make the company look good to the inside world, the executives, and higher ups.

Playing fast and loose with cash flow and sales, finance and accounting are masters at juggling figures on a spreadsheet. Every built-in formula to make the numbers black is their friend. If desperate, they can always work with IT to rig spreadsheets to always show a profit.

Accounting and finance can't get away with wearing funny costumes when they have to present the dire picture to the C-suite. They have to be stoic and calm in the face of lashings and beatings. Some have learned to tap dance, or do the soft shoe, or sing an aria from a tragic opera, to lighten up meetings with irate executives. Some have been known to wear tuxedos and top hats and put on white gloves to deliver particularly damaging budgets.

Their motto is, "It's better to entertain executives than tell them the truth."

The accounting types are annoyed by the noise coming out of marketing. The marketing folks think the accounting department are unfriendly, maybe even boring. The accounting team thinks the marketing people are noisy and disruptive. They complain about each other to HR. They might even argue in the halls. They're a perfect dysfunctional match, always at odds with each other, and a recipe for office conflict. Conflict and tension are what make the world go round at the dysfunctional company.

If it makes sense to put related departments together, don't do it. Departments should be haphazardly scattered around the building in places that don't make sense. It should be inconvenient to get from point A to point B. This makes sure nothing gets done.

Remote employees might think they're free of all this office nonsense. They can't escape it either. It's live and in color on their laptop screens, as departments take pot shots at each other in chats and e-mails. They can even jump in on the fun from the comfort of their home without worrying about being hit by flying objects. In the office, they might get hit by a flying stapler or a loose portable hard drive flung over a cubicle divider.

Desk Defense for Securing the PAWS:
De-Desking and the Office Homeless

Every employee will have to defend their PAWS at some point from threats on all fronts. These include hostile auditors, HR, executives or even just employees from other departments looking for information.

Building a fort around the PAWS may not be feasible, but there are other defenses the threatened employee can implement.

Every employee should learn how to make crude weapons of mass destruction from office supplies. Catapults for hurling spit balls or small candy can be made of rubber bands and tape dispensers.

Staple removers can be placed like landmines around the PAWS as a trap. Pens and pencils can be used as spears or, combined with rubber bands, into projectiles like desk-based short-range missiles.

When things get really tough, and guerrilla warfare is required, makeshift stink bombs can be crafted in the bathroom. Toilet paper, when available, since it's often in short supply at the dysfunctional company, can be wadded up and dunked in the frequently clogged toilet bowls. These can be hurled across several rows of cubicles for greater effect, like **Inter Row Ballistic Missiles (IRBM)**. They have a longer range than the catapults just mentioned.

Whatever the weapon of choice, the well-prepared employee is armed and ready for any bureaucratic intrusion.

Every employee should dread the day when they're **de-desked**. This is the process of being forcibly evicted from your PAWS. Those homeless people begging in the hallway; they're not really homeless. They're employees who have lost their PAWS and haven't been reassigned.

With frequent unannounced reorganizations and incessant shuffling of management, the employee will eventually be de-desked.

Employees will know de-desking is imminent when someone from facilities management suddenly shows up at their PAWS and rudely tells them they're being moved. There is no advance notice. It just happens. They aren't even polite or nice about it. They're followed by burly people with boxes, who tell the employee to pack up – right now.

Nothing is as much fun as being de-desked right in the middle of the day, especially while trying to – imagine the unimaginable — to get work done. It's very humiliating to be thrown into the hall with their laptops, duffle bags and water bottles, and all their other swag.

The confused employee has no choice but to comply. Otherwise, they may be banished to an Area of Total Darkness (to be discussed shortly), a sign they will be soon shown the door.

Related to de-desking is the concept euphemistically called "hoteling." To save space, road warriors who rarely come into the office, aren't given a fixed PAWS. Instead, they have to reserve an empty cubicle or desk.

Calling them "hotels" is an understatement. They don't even have room service, a bathroom or a refreshment cooler. Clean areas with sheets turned down with a chocolate treat on the pillow? Clean towels? No way. More like a like dirty cubicle with candy and gum wrappers left from the last occupant. Maybe even a chewed up sticky gift under the seat.

The catch is that they're the worst work spaces in the office – in noisy areas, dark corners, behind pillars, or even right in the middle of the lunch room, where people walk by and make fun of them. Employee humiliation comes in many forms at the dysfunctional company, and no one is immune.

Free Fire Zones (FFZ) and Areas of Total Darkness (ATD)

Beyond the employee's PAWS, there should be **Free Fire Zones (FFZ)** strategically scattered around the office in accessible locations. This is an open area in one corner of the office, typically at least on every floor, marked off by spray paint or barbed wire and a sign with an inverted yellow triangle at the entrance.

Employees can freely scream or bang their head against the wall in these areas without fear of reprisals, or fear of HR putting a report in their personnel file. These are like a gym, or workout room, where employees can take out their many frustrations from work, or attempts at work, at the dysfunctional company.

Yoga and meditation aren't allowed in FFZs, since they would alleviate employee stress. Since these zones are audit and HR free, the **No Yoga Policy** is enforced through signs posted on the walls warning: "Yoga not allowed here."

This is the source of the moaning noises often heard in the background in dysfunctional company offices. It's not unusual to see employees walking around the office with bruises on their foreheads from frequently banging their head on the wall.

Remote employees have the luxury of designating an area in their work location for their FFZ. This could be a closet, where the employee can lock themselves in and vent their frustrations during the day. Another cool idea is to throw a chair through a window when work inevitably go sideways. Yelling at the spouse and kids, or kicking the family pet, are also good stress relievers for remote employees.

A good survival mechanism is the **Reverse Elbow Curl** (**REC**, pronounced like "wreck, as in "train wreck"). This can be done at the employee's PAWS instead of in an FFZ. In this maneuver, the employee makes a fist with each hand and bends their arms back, reaching as far as possible behind their head. The employee then opens their mouth and makes a silent scream (see Figure 2).

This is an effective stress reliever that can be done quietly at the PAWS without bothering neighbors. Employees seen doing RECs at their PAWS can always just say they're doing a "wreck." It's also safer than throwing things, like furniture or office supplies, which could injure fellow employees or nick up cubicles.

Beyond FFZs are **Areas of Total Darkness (ATD)**. These are open spaces that appear as the office shrinks from multiple layoffs. They are eerie areas without PAWS, formerly inhabited by employees, only now scarred like a battlefield after a war, littered with remains of office furniture and broken computer screens. Dark and silent, the employee may be tempted to seek refuge from the chaos in the office in ATDs. Here they can meditate or wonder in amazement at the wreckage left by the dysfunctional company.

Figure 2
Reverse Elbow Curl

***An employee doing a Reverse Elbow Curl
or "wreck"***

Note: This photo was taken in the morning, since only one head wound is visible. The employee probably sustained the injury in a TWM the first thing in the morning or during a morning break in an FFZ.

The Employee Life Cycle: From Hiring to Firing

Employees at the dysfunctional company should be treated like perishable produce. They're fresh when first picked, go through a clearly defined lifecycle, during which they're ground up into a slush and then poured down the drain.

Employees, again, like perishables, should always have an expiration date. After this date, they can be let go, or in coded company jargon – Company Speak from Habit Three -- "relieved of their responsibilities." These dates are a secret, kept in shadowy personnel files only available to HR people with a Top-Secret clearance. Like other departments in the dysfunctional company, HR is full of cliques jealously guarding their turfs, hiding information from each other.

When the time comes, as will be seen shortly, the expiration date is revealed, and the employee is out the door.

Ideally, unsuspecting candidates are plucked like ripe fruit right out of school by campus recruiters. They're young and full of enthusiasm, seduced by slick marketing campaigns, showing the dysfunctional company would be a cool place to work. There might even be an offer of a "management training program" with promises of regular advancement.

These are bogus programs where unwitting employees get tossed around like a beach ball from department to department, and office to office, until they reach a certain level of management and then "top out," so to speak. They reach a plateau both in rank and salary. Most never reach the executive level promised to them when they joined the program.

After the employee has been at the dysfunctional company many years, they settle in and think they're comfortable. They get good at what they do, maybe even develop an expertise known company-wide, and the work becomes routine. They get regular pay increases and generous company benefits, if available. They get integrated into the tribal structure of the company and learn the secret rituals – the hand signs and facial gestures – of their particular clique. They feel like, or think they feel like, they're at home.

Then suddenly one day the Angel of Layoffs appears at the employee's PAWS. Their expiration date had come up on HR's calendar, and they were marked for removal. Then the rinse and wash cycle starts all over again. A young recruit, fresh out of school, and full of excitement and energy now inhabits the deposed employee's PAWS. And, it goes unsaid, since HR would never admit it, they're working at a fraction of the salary of the old employee.

Little does the young recruit realize, someday, years down the road, the same fate awaits them.

Employee Metrics and Annual Performance Reviews

Employees need to be evaluated regularly in a process called "Performance Reviews," an annual rite of passage like the Ides of March. If their company offers an annual bonus, they will be told how tiny a sliver of the pie, if any, they will receive (see Figure 3).

Employees should be reduced to numbers, which can be boiled down into a set of metrics for measuring performance. The process should be impersonal and cold and not involve any intuition or evaluation of the employee as a person.

Employees should be treated like objects that can be packaged and quantified and thrown into a spreadsheet for review. The employee's strengths and weaknesses and where they might fit best in the company should never be a factor in their review. In fact, if possible, every employee's name should be replaced with a number. This gives HR additional tools for locating – or hunting down like

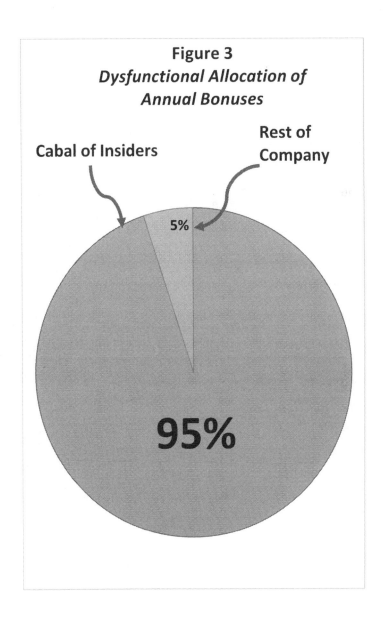

Figure 3
Dysfunctional Allocation of Annual Bonuses

Cabal of Insiders

Rest of Company

5%

95%

big game in the jungle – employees besides just their bar code.

The best way to track employee activity, and use it later to hang the employee during the annual review, is the time-honored and lowly time sheet.

Time sheets must be filled in every week, and employees should be threatened with dismissal, if they're not completed on time. The day time sheets are due, employees should be hounded and harassed by e-mail, as a reminder, as if they don't already get enough e-mail.

As expected at the dysfunctional company, the IT system hosting the time sheet application will go down on the day they're due. Whether the system crashed because everybody is doing them at once, or just because the system is outdated and sucks, doesn't matter. The time sheets haven't been submitted on time, and managers will start screaming.

Time sheets can then be converted into the precise metrics needed for the annual review.

The following is a sample of buckets that should be the staple of every time sheet:

- **UBA** – Unproductive Bureaucratic Activity
- **USA** – Unproductive Social Activities

- **BAR** – Bathroom Attendance Ratio (time spent in bathroom breaks)
- **MAR** – Meeting Attendance Ratio (percent of the day in meetings)

The ideal employee will have a high UBA and USA, a low BAR, and a high MAR (see Figure 4).

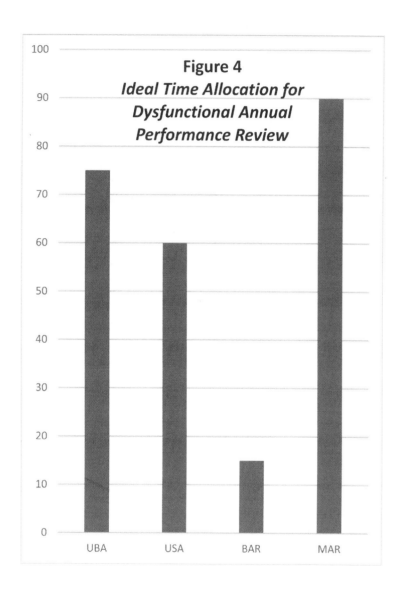

Figure 4
Ideal Time Allocation for Dysfunctional Annual Performance Review

That means they're tied up in bureaucratic bullshit or forced socializing, take few bathroom breaks, if any, and are in meetings most of the day.

These numbers and a set of nebulous goals should be presented to the employee during a face-to-face meeting with the employee's supervisor.

A sample of dysfunctional goals might include the following:
- Attitude – "You need to adjust your attitude. You're too positive."
- Work Ethic – "You work too hard. This has to stop."
- Community – "You don't fit in here. You have too many good ideas for the business."
- Team Work – "You get things done. Management frowns down on that."

At the conclusion of the meeting, the employee should be told their annual bonus figure. The employee should be made to feel the dysfunctional company was generous, even though their share is like a pimple on an elephant (Figure 3), compared to what the CEO and the Cabal of Insiders take home.

How to Properly Discipline Uncooperative Employees

Every employee at the dysfunctional company will eventually need to be disciplined. Hemmed in by so many rules and procedures, it's almost impossible not to get into trouble.

Employees can be disciplined in three ways: the victim of an audit finding, summoned to HR to be scolded and lectured, or by a letter put in their personnel file.

Two typical scenarios for audit are, either being summoned by audit into a conference room to undergo brutal interrogation, as has already been discussed, or secondly, being arrested by audit goons at the employee's PAWS.

An arrest by audit happens when employees hear a message over the office loudspeaker, sounding something like: "Attention, Audit! There is a policy violation in process at cubicle 23C. Repeat. Audit, please proceed immediately to cubicle 23C. A policy violation is in progress."

Neighboring employees will see auditors wearing armbands and clutching laptops running through the hall to the accused's cubicle. They may look like Olympic speed skaters, crouched down, arms flying left and right, racing between cubicles.

It's very important for employees to keep calm and just ignore the commotion. It's been known for difficult employees to fight laptop-armed auditors in the halls, trying in vain to resist. Some may kick and scream, or bite their captors. It won't stop them. Audit will always win.

If they can't pin down the accused, they will blow a whistle and more auditors will come to help. Eventually, there will be a swarm of auditors, like a hornet's nest, and the offender will be subdued. If necessary, a pile of auditors may sit on top of the employee, maybe even form a human pyramid, to keep him or her down on the ground.

Employees sitting at their PAWS know better than to interfere. They may see or hear a scuffle in front of their PAWS. It might disturb their concentration. But at no point should they intervene. They have to keep doing whatever they're doing, whatever it is: work, non-work, streaming adult movies on their laptop, or just bureaucratic support activities. An employee caught trying to save another employee from kidnap by audit will be the subject of an audit finding themselves. Interfering with audit is a crime punishable by banishment to a remote company office in a location without running water or indoor plumbing.

Employees summoned to HR, on the other hand, for lashings and lectures, face milder punishments. An HR representative will summon them to the office over the loudspeaker. "Will So-And-So please proceed to HR immediately. You are being summoned to HR. If you do not proceed immediately, you will be detained and brought to HR by Security. Your presence is required."

The HR representative will meet them at the door and escort them to a private office. The HR rep then closes the door and rolls up a newspaper and says, "Bad employee. Sit in the corner. Poo on the paper, not on your desk." The embarrassed employee will be lectured about some trivial misdeed and sent back to their PAWS. Trivial misdeeds could range from using unapproved office supplies to giving a finger to an executive while sober at a company-approved forced socializing event.

If the matter is serious enough, HR will put a letter in the employee's personnel file. Disciplinary letters are kept secret and are only brought out when needed during future HR torture sessions to discredit the employee further. This is all part of the paper trail used to get rid of a problem employee (free thinkers, innovators, talented individuals, etc.) or to eject an employee whose expiration date has passed.

Even in the dysfunctional company, there are rules and procedures for liquidating employees.

Employee Removal Procedures and Rituals

All good things must come to an end. The roller coaster ride called the dysfunctional company goes up and down and from side to side and then goes in circles, before finally stopping to unceremoniously fling employees into the air.

Employees can exit the dysfunctional company either voluntarily or involuntarily. This Habit deals with employees who are involuntarily removed. Those with the foresight to leave on their own avoid the humiliation of being laid off.

Drilling further down in the Art of Involuntary Employee Removal, employees can be let go either individually or en masse. Individuals can be laid off for cause – not decorating their PAWS with enough company-branded paraphernalia, using unapproved sticky notes or for having a progressive idea for the business – or if they've reached their expiration date.

It's rare for an employee to survive long enough at the dysfunctional company to reach retirement. So many things could go wrong: their department could be cut, they might go insane during a meeting, get a fatal skin rash from a vending machine snack, get runover by a security patrol in the parking lot or simply succumb to a mortal wound in an FFZ.

For employees axed for cause, the company first builds a case against the employee. Their manager and HR will conspire together to dredge up any evidence of wrongdoing, fabricated or real, to trap the employee. They will dig through secret personnel files, pull up past performance reviews and surveillance tapes of the employee's activities in bathrooms and breakrooms.

Once the evidence has been assembled, the employee's supervisor then presents the target with a Performance Improvement Program (PIP). As discussed in Habit Three, this is just fancy Company Speak for putting the employee on probation. The PIP will probably have unreachable goals for an employee targeted for destruction long ago.

The dysfunctional company then has elaborate rituals for assassinating the offending employee. It might be something like a vice president from the home office, who normally never visits the local office, appearing bright and early on a Monday morning. This is a sign of bloodshed yet to come.

Employees should pay close attention to these rituals, especially if the executive conducting the executions is carrying a bloody razor blade or switch blade out in the open. This usually means someone has already been axed – literally – and that there may be more to follow. Employees need to wear galoshes, or at least be careful, to not slip on pools of blood on the floor.

First, the employee's supervisor delivers the news. The employee is then marched down to HR and is shaken down in the "exit interview." This is where the employee is forced to sign a pile of paperwork. This includes documents relinquishing their right to sue the company and a Non-Compete Agreement, saying they won't take any customers to either a future employer, dysfunctional or otherwise, or to their own business.

Last, security escorts the disgraced employee to the lobby in handcuffs. Another HR rep waiting at the door will rip the epaulets off the employee's shoulder and then crack his or her laptop over their knee before brusquely shoving the employee through the revolving door.

The removed employee can take heart that countless others have passed through the same revolving door, The Revolving Door of Shame, a symbol of the dysfunctional company's layoff practices.

The dysfunctional company has also other touching rituals for liquidating employees and executives offsite. These might include having the HR executioner meet the target at the airport as they're about to board a flight for a business trip, or delivering the news in the middle of lunch at a fancy restaurant. It shows real class to have everybody order their food, then fold their menus and then be told they've been fired.

Nothing beats being humiliated in public in front of strangers by someone from the office bearing bad news.

Mass Layoffs and Death Panels

As for massive employee removals, the question of who shall live and who shall die is critical.

The dysfunctional company should have executives assigned to a permanent **Death Panel**, which has lists of candidates targeted for bureaucratic assassination. This list should be updated regularly with few names removed but new names constantly added. The list can then be either partially or fully activated by either the Cabal, or executives they delegate to do the job, at the appropriate time.

The Death Panel, obviously, should have its own secret office behind closed doors. The door should only be marked with a guillotine to indicate to employees this is a no-go zone.

A handy way for the dysfunctional company to decide which employees to weed out is the **Executive Equivalency Multiplier Factor (EEMF**, pronounced "EE-muf"). This is the compensation of an executive measured as a multiple of the average salary of an employee. For example, if executive deadwood, which should have been put out to pasture during the last mass layoff, is making the equivalent of the salary of 200 employees, the EEMF is 200.

It would make sense to dump the poorly performing executive, instead of 200 valuable employees, since the cost savings would be the same. Instead, the dysfunctional company dumps the 200 useful employees and keeps the executive door stop. Again, raw political power and brute force are what rule the dysfunctional company, not common sense or the value of employees.

Generally, the dysfunctional company uses the It Rolls Downhill Rule to determine the number of employees to let go. This is where a member of the Cabal of Insiders throws a thunderbolt down from a mountain top with a percentage, say, fifteen percent. Then that number rolls down the hierarchy until it hits bottom. The lowest manager on the totem pole must then belly up to the bar with the names of who to remove.

It's never really clear where the Cabal of Insiders gets its number. It's probably just a guess based on the bogus budget cooked up by accounting and finance. They get their numbers throwing darts at a dartboard at their favorite bar after work and then just fabricate the rest of the figures based on erroneous assumptions.

Another cool thing the dysfunctional company does is send employees home for the day and tells them they will receive an e-mail with their "status." In the meantime, their access to systems is cut off while they wait for the big news. The downside is that by announcing a **Go Home Day**, management is tipping its hat that a massive layoff is afoot. There is nothing more heartwarming then to be laid off by e-mail.

The most fun layoffs are when there is an element of surprise. Employees come to work, either to the office or remote, and are suddenly let go during the day, without notice, right while they might be trying to do some work, or whatever passes as work. The element of surprise is lost with a Go Home Day.

Uniformed security details then comb the office, plucking up impacted employees from their PAWS. Employees might be pulled right out of meetings or have their laptops closed brusquely in the middle of the lewd movie they might be streaming.

They are then marched down to HR, in full view of the survivors, who gawk at them, grateful this isn't their last day – yet. They will be given large envelopes full of "exit" documents, given a box lunch with a fortune cookie that says, "Good luck in your job search," and escorted out of the building to the parking lot.

Remote employees have a similar experience, except virtually. They will be e-mailed their exit papers, which will include instructions on how to return their laptop to the company mother ship, and then their screens will go dark.

Keeping Dead Employees at Their Desks

A popular slogan at dysfunctional companies is "Work hard, play hard." This usually means "Work hard, drop dead."

Some employees who do actual work may suddenly pass out, or even drop dead, at their desk or PAWS from exhaustion. These employees should be propped up in their chair and left upright. They should be put on display in the office. They serve as an example to passing employees what can happen when they do productive work. Dead employees didn't follow the HR rule to use the REC to relieve stress. This is an important lesson.

The sight of dead employees propped up at their desks will scare other employees who might be considering doing anything useful at the company. They will learn that it's better to go to an FFZ and scream, or do a "wreck" at their desk, or put a pin with a company logo in a voodoo doll (also with the company logo) than keep trying to get anything done at the dysfunctional company.

It might be hard to tell if a remote employee has dropped dead. After a while, the lack of e-mail activity, or missing mandatory meetings, are signs they have no pulse. One thought is to have pulse monitors sent to remote employees. They can plug these into their laptops, where their vital signs are monitored and recorded for review by audit.

In these situations, a skull and cross bones should be put over their messaging icon, indicating to employees online that the employee has passed. This macabre image serves the same purpose – to frighten employees online into staying clear of anything resembling productive activity. The company surveillance software can also be configured to check for employees dropping dead remotely.

The employee may be remote but they will learn they could meet the same fate as their dearly departed office-bound colleagues.

At some point, the deceased employee will start to decompose. Row Captains should be responsible for removal of corpses in their area and cleaning up the mess. Row captains will need to be able to tell the difference between the living dead working at their desks, and those who have already checked out and left for that great dysfunctional company in the sky.

The dysfunctional company offers training to sharpen this skill and, in fact, may require it for all Row Captains. Not taking this course should be noted in the offending Row Captain's personnel file, marked against their performance review and then, of course, be an audit finding for the department.

The stary-eyed recruit, who had no idea what he or she would be in for, has been sucked into the vortex known as the dysfunctional company.

Habit Seven:
The Company Doesn't Serve the Common Good

"Who cares if it doesn't work?
Let's get it out there as fast as possible,
then fix it later after customers complain."

Habit Seven:
The Company Doesn't Serve the Common Good

"Screw the contract. We can always sue later."

The dysfunctional company is only out for itself. It's all about self-preservation. When the world closes in, the dysfunctional company fights back. It isn't in the business of serving the public or the common good. Sometimes, as has been seen throughout this book, it isn't even in the business of doing business either. It's just a platform for money and power for its people at the top.

If it can't even serve its employees and customers, it can't serve the community, or the outside world.

The dysfunctional company doesn't take kindly to criticism from outsiders. When attacked, it defends. It fights back with gooey advertising, slick public relations campaigns or, when really backed into a corner, fierce lawsuits. When that doesn't work, they spend money to influence legislation. If the law doesn't work for the dysfunctional company, pay someone to make it work.

The same double-speak it uses within the company, it uses with the media, in rare moments when it agrees to talk to outsiders.

It's always somebody else's fault. The problem must be out there. It isn't in here. It couldn't be us. Our product or service is perfect. Our people, especially our executive team, are beyond reproach. It must be bad apples in the community, stirring up trouble.

We, the dysfunctional company, are good. They, the public, are bad. The dysfunctional company projects the same us-versus-them mentality within the company to the outside world.

The dysfunctional company ignores changes in society affecting its product or service. They don't apply to us. We're above all that. We can keep doing what we're doing, even if it doesn't work, even if customers aren't buying our product or service anymore.

If the dysfunctional company can't transform itself from within, because it's become too bureaucratic and stodgy, it can't be expected to transform itself for the outside world.

The dysfunctional company never looks within. Maybe it's a bad product or service. Maybe bad management. Maybe bad marketing. Maybe bad hiring practices, or hiring the wrong people. Maybe bad customer service. Maybe too much bureaucracy. Maybe too many little dictators fighting each other. Maybe no strategy, or a bad strategy, or bad execution of something resembling strategy, or a good strategy mashed up by the dysfunctional company's turf wars and bureaucracy, resulting in all the above.

Or maybe just an outdated product and brand outflanked by competitors more in touch with its customers and reality.

It's better to lash out at the public and the community. Somehow the dysfunctional company is just misunderstood. It just doesn't get enough love.

Can Any Company Serve the Common Good?

Any company is in business to make money. That's just a simple fact. The bigger question is whether a company can both make money and help people, or help its community. This is one of those great philosophical questions of the universe beyond the scope of this book.

For the dysfunctional company, it doesn't matter if the question can be answered. The dysfunctional company can't even answer basic questions about what it does every day, let alone big questions beyond itself.

As has been seen until now through the last six habits, when the only questions being asked in the dysfunctional company are "Where is that lost expense report?" "Where are my sticky notes" or "What is our marketing strategy?" or "Do we even have any strategy, at all?" or "Why isn't anybody buying our product anymore?" it's too consumed by its own bullshit to move forward or, in fact, to move anywhere except nowhere.

Serving the community, or the common good, becomes an afterthought.

Mission Statements: Our Mission is to Screw You

The purpose of a business – any business – is to make money. Period. A company may say it's serving a higher cause. It may say it's about helping people. It may even say it's about serving customers. It may say a bunch of pie-in-the-sky feel-good things in public. In the end, it's all about making money. Everything else is just talk.

If the dysfunctional company were honest about itself, which it isn't, it would admit this and be done with it. Instead, the dysfunctional company does what it does best. It puts more energy into

writing bogus mission statements in complicated
Company Speak to confuse the public than in
building the business and pursuing customers.

There is only one mission statement for any
company:
"We're in business to make money."

The dysfunctional mission statement goes further:
"We're in business to make money, even if it's at
the expense of our customers and employees."

The dysfunctional mission statement might just as
well say, in addition:
"Our mission is to screw you."

Another honest mission statement for the
dysfunctional company would be:
"Our business isn't your business. We're not in the
business of keeping promises."

The dysfunctional company then prominently
displays these works of art in their lobby for the
world to see. Employees coming in every morning
just ignore them. It's not because they eventually
stop noticing them. It's because the rot they
experience inside the door doesn't match the
mission statement outside the door.

Poor Communication Inside Leads to
Poor Communication Outside

Just as the dysfunctional company deceives its employees and management – and ultimately, itself – through poor communication, as was seen in Habit Three, it deceives the public. The idiotic mission statement at the entrance is just the beginning.

Poor communication internally can't help but leak out as unadulterated bullshit to the outside world. Just as it says one thing to its own people, and does something else, it says one thing to the public, and does something else. Deceptive advertising and marketing are a high art for the dysfunctional company.

The dysfunctional company's propaganda machines would be the envy of any petty dictator.

It's equally as important for the Cabal of Insiders, especially the CEO, to be as out of touch with the community and the outside world as they are with their own dysfunctional company.

The dysfunctional company says it cares about the environment, then continues to pollute and contribute to climate change. It may even have a huge public relations campaign with celebrity endorsements as a smoke screen, about how "clean" or "green" or "carbon-neutral" the company is. The pictures shown in the campaign clearly weren't taken at the dysfunctional company's filthy plants damaging the environment.

The dysfunctional company is a master at slashing and burning communities. It comes in like a carpet bagger, sets up shop – a business, an office, a warehouse or a plant – and then just as quickly shuts down and moves out, sometimes suddenly, sometimes without notice, boarding up a town and trashing its employees.

The dysfunctional company says employees come first. It may even go further and say it cares about its employees. It says its employees are its best resources, and on and on and on, ad nauseum. "Employees come first." "Employees are our number one priority."

It may even show smiling employees hard at work in well-choreographed advertisements in beautifully staged facilities and offices. Then it conducts mass layoffs the next day. The employees in the advertisements? They had no idea what was coming. The layoffs had been planned long before filming started.

Remember those handsome hunks and gorgeous babes in the ads from Habit Five? The well-dressed and happy employees marched in front of the camera are just more of the same. This is just the employee version of the satisfaction faked by customers in product advertising.

The dysfunctional company gives with one hand and then takes with another. After stealing the souls of its employees, it spreads its rot to the community by preying on its customers. If all else fails, the dysfunctional company can sue or, even better, push for legislation to change the laws altogether.

Business by Lawsuit:
Our Quality Control is Customer Complaints

Lawsuits for the dysfunctional company are a form of risk analysis. For the dysfunctional company, risk analysis is figuring out whether the settlement from a lawsuit for a defective product or service is cheaper than fixing the defect. If it's easier to settle a suit than fix it in the factory, or the office, then go to court.

Lawsuits are a natural outcome of the sloppy way the dysfunctional company does business. It's more important to get a product or service out the door as fast as possible than to test it, or check if it works, or do market research or focus groups before launch. Quality control is following up on customer complaints after the product or service has been released, not before. Better to have customer complaints afterward, than do a quality review beforehand.

No news is good news at the dysfunctional company. If they don't complain, the product or service works. If they complain, ignore them. Let the damage fester until someone gets hurt and they sue.

Sometimes, it seems the dysfunctional company is always either being sued or filing suits. When the dysfunctional company isn't being sued, it can sue its competitors. The dysfunctional company would rather do business by lawsuit than through hard work, claiming infringement over this or that. It's much easier to sue competitors than to innovate or produce anything of value anybody would want.

Forced Charities,
Forced Lobbying,
Shrinking Benefits

The dysfunctional company loves telling the world how it's a good citizen and how it gives back to the community. It does this by forcing it's employees to be its frontpeople for an array of public charities, all approved and sponsored by the dysfunctional company, of course.

Among all the other crap foisted on employees all day long, they're hounded to give to charities. They're herded into conference rooms in the middle of the day, while they're trying to work, to watch recorded presentations about this or that charitable organization. For the company, it's positive publicity, or maybe a tax break. It's not really about altruism or guilt – the dysfunctional company has neither.

For employees, it's just one more distraction. The dysfunctional company would rather give to charities than give to its own employees, who watch their benefits shrink from year to year. Charitable donations are up, but contributions to health insurance are down.

Some of these charities are worthwhile and provide services employees might use some day. Others may be of no interest or use to an employee, at all, or the employee may already be working with a charitable organization on their own outside of work. The point isn't the value of the charities, but that the company coerces employees into donating, whether they like it or not.

The same goes for lobbying. When there is proposed legislation affecting the company, employees are herded back into conference rooms.

They're told how critical this legislation is for the company and, possibly, even their jobs. More likely, the proposal would cut the insane income of the Cabal in their ivory tower or negatively impact the already shrinking benefits of the peasants in their PAWS.

Employees are urged to call their legislators and are given a detailed script with instructions. The employee is told not to veer from the script, or face some unspecified punishment.

Employees are told, of course, this is all voluntary. They're told no one will know whether or not they give, nor how much they donate. They're told no one will know if they called their legislator. Then, after the charity or lobbying campaign has passed, they wonder why their supervisor calls them in and reprimands them for not donating, or not lobbying. How did their supervisor know?

It's not a mystery.

The dysfunctional company knows everything – and not just about its employees.

Privacy? We Know All About You

The dysfunctional company gathers as much data as possible, from as many sources as possible, from the customers it loathes so much. Meanwhile, it sends out a "privacy policy" to all its customers in print tinier than a flea written in dense legalese unintelligible to human life.

Then, one fine sunny day, for some unknown reason, there is a data breach. The confused customer wonders how this could have happened when they were told the company has first-rate cutting-edge super-duper military-grade security systems.

The dysfunctional company now sends out a follow up letter, advising there was a data breach and their personal information may have been stolen. Typical of its backhanded double-speak, the letter says, "But we don't think any of your sensitive data was among what was taken." The dazed customer now wonders why they're then being offered identity theft protection, if nothing 'sensitive' was taken.

Of course, in the twisted world of dysfunctional communication, they can't say "hacked," which is what really happened. They have to sugar coat with the innocuous-sounding wording "data breach."

When Cabals Go Criminal:
The Dysfunctional Goes Rogue

When the dysfunctional company goes totally off the rails, its Cabal of Insiders may be tempted to go rogue. Sometimes, they become criminals. Not surprisingly, using twisted logic, some play victim or martyr. "I had to do it. It was the only way I could save the company." Not surprisingly, delusional leadership is part of the dysfunctional company. Criminality comes naturally. It's just the next step.

They forgot the purpose of executives is to lead, not steal. They forgot how to run a business above ground, not into the ground.

Others don't even pretend to be good. They just steal and embezzle without thinking, and then try to cover it up or worse, frame someone else in the company. Eventually their sticky hands get caught in the till.

Sadly, Cabal wrongdoers never really get punished. They end up in cushy prisons, more like a resort, where they work on their suntan by the pool or get tennis lessons to work on their backhand. They just bide their time, don't make waves, and in a few years, they're back on the street ready to terrorize another company, maybe at an even higher level with even more perks than before.

The lesson they learn inside the joint: Crime pays.

No e-mails. No meetings. No phone calls. For the disgraced former executive, it's like a government-funded vacation. What could be a better?

For them, prison is better than working, and it sure beats being in the office. Of course, the damage they caused, and the destroyed lives they left behind, rarely recover. Their abandoned co-workers are often still imprisoned at the dysfunctional company – if it survived. And if it didn't, leaving some without work, those are just the breaks. The dysfunctional company, rogue or straight, is heartless.

Onwards and Upward in Disserve to the Community

Besides being a disservice to the wider community through its actions, the dysfunctional company also bequeaths to the world twisted graduates of its hallowed halls of poor management. Graduates move on to damage other companies, disrupt government as incompetent officials or become ineffective regulators in their industry.

Some may even go into politics, where they can inflict the same pain they caused at their dysfunctional companies on the public. Former executives of the dysfunctional company make great politicians. Many have already been broken in through years of creative schmoozing and socializing at the right times in the right places – exactly like politicians.

The most incompetent are mere diplomats or figureheads – not businesspeople – with little upstairs and few accomplishments. But they sure still clean up well when shaved and coiffed. They only got ahead on their charms and good looks. They worked their way up through a lot of handshakes and cocktail parties – again, just like politicians.

In fact, politics is the perfect place for dysfunctional company graduates and alumni to hang their hat as the last stop in their colorful careers wrecking companies and lives. The thinking is: "If you can't do anything else, go into politics." They can indulge in their worst power fantasies.

If they become legislators, for example, they can do the same thing they did at their former dysfunctional company – ignore complaints from the public. Legislative proposals often arise from customer complaints to legislators about problems created by the dysfunctional company. Just as they proved incapable of resolving these problems at their former company, they can now prove themselves equally incapable of drafting legislation to resolve those same problems for the wider world.

If they can't be legislators, they buy legislators. When the dysfunctional company can't change laws, it buys laws in its favor through expensive lobbyists. The dysfunctional company is a master at throwing money around to get what it wants most – legal cover to screw its customers and the public. Just as power and politics are all that count within the dysfunctional company, politics and money and influence are all that count when dealing with outsiders. Better to bully than appear weak. A legislator in the pocket is worth more than two retired executives in the bush.

If they become regulators, on the other hand, they can create other, non-legislative, obstacles to doing business through excessive and unnecessary rules and regulations. Instead of just erecting barriers within their company, they can now build even higher roadblocks to business outside the dysfunctional company. They can peddle their "expertise" in their field, leveraging their cutting-edge knowledge screwing up their prior dysfunctional company to now hollow out its entire industry.

Layers upon layers of regulators, battling over jurisdictions and responsibilities, is a mirror image of the turf battles within the dysfunctional company. There is nothing like bolting an external bureaucracy onto the internal bureaucracy of a struggling dysfunctional company already on life support to choke the life out of it.

Becoming industry regulators is the perfect resting place for recovering auditors who have left the dysfunctional company with their sanity intact. Other ex-auditors, unfortunately, aren't so lucky. Some become emotional cripples. Others have ended up in straightjackets or padded cells in mental hospitals. Just one too many findings was all it took to throw them off the cliff of insanity.

The dysfunctional company creates these outstanding future leaders for disserving the community through its **Asshole Management Development Training Program (AMDTP,** pronounced AM-dee-tep, with the emphasis on the "AM," and "dee" pronounced like the letter "D").

The Asshole Management Development Training Program (AMDTP)

The AMDTP is an exclusive club within the dysfunctional company. In fact, only a dysfunctional company would even have such a program. Someone must carry on the tradition of the Cabal of Insiders until the ship sinks, and the

AMDTP is the best way to pass the torch to the next arsonist.

The dysfunctional company is ideal for the AMDTP. The toxic culture and work environment at the dysfunctional company is already a natural breeding ground for producing deranged and ineffective executives and managers.

Candidates need to be carefully selected by HR and then approved by executive management before they can learn the secret handshake and forbidden rituals, and the right scent of incense to burn, for membership in the AMDTP elite.

In true dysfunctional style, the selection process for the AMDTP is convoluted and full of useless exercises and activities that have no bearing on the candidate's actual skills or fitness for management and leadership.

The screening process should start with personality tests, like those described in Habit Six about employee recruitment. Since those tests, as already mentioned, are cryptic and inaccurate, simply generating incomprehensible – and irrelevant – strings of letters, they're the ideal first step in the dysfunctional process.

After that, they go through a series of interviews with higher ups, maybe write essays about why they're seeking this promotion, and what they would do in the new position. To round out the candidate's profile, they may also be asked to write about their hobbies and outside interests, or even their community activities.

Outside activities, particularly those for the community, need to be chosen carefully to send the right signal to upper management. The ideal candidate must be pliable, so he or she can be easily manipulated by the Cabal, yet still have the intestinal fortitude to act independently to do what is necessary to carry on the mission of the dysfunctional company – keep employees down and screw customers.

Golfing is an example of a good outside activity, since it shows the candidate will be able to hobnob after hours or, maybe during long lunches, with his or her new executive peers. This has been known to sometimes require drinking. The candidate should have a liver function test as part of their AMDTP application to make sure they can still stand while inebriated for 18 holes. In fact, there should be check box in the evaluation paperwork, "Can this candidate hold their alcohol?"

Gardening is negative, since the only garden the candidate's future peers harvest is their investment portfolios and personal bank accounts. It's not macho enough, and too wimpy, for the dog-eat-dog dysfunctional company. It also usually doesn't involve drinking or sexual harassment, two key traits for aspiring AMDTPs.

Volunteering at a homeless shelter, or helping refugees, are other examples of negative activities, since they indicate the candidate is a do-gooder. Do-gooders don't do well in the ruthless and competitive atmosphere of the dysfunctional company. They're too team-oriented.

Executive screeners are looking for individuals who will participate in important outside activities: heavy drinking and, in the case of straight male candidates, skirt chasing and other male-bonding rituals. Anything that favors the "old-boy" – literally all male – network is a plus in the dysfunctional company. The dysfunctional company is stuck in a past where sexism was the norm, and the men, and only the men, always got their way. The Cabal of Insiders, if all male, is like a frat house anyways. The alpha male candidate should fit in perfectly.

They also look for those who won't rock the boat or threaten their power. They're especially on the lookout for potential whistle-blowers, who might try to take down the whole sand castle.

Candidates for promotions at any company must always be screened, of course. Every company, dysfunctional or not, has a promotion process with required steps. Except in the dysfunctional company, positive attributes and skills required for the post are ignored in favor of personalities. The whole process is just a lot of paper shuffling and tap dancing. It's all about "fit" – not for clothing – to use another popular term from Company Speak (remember Company Speak from Habit Three?). The question becomes: Will this candidate "fit" into our screwed-up culture?

After all the paperwork and interviews have been completed, HR will assign the candidate an Asshole Potential Index (API), a score ranging from 0, the lowest, to 10, the highest, to determine eligibility for the AMDTP. The threshold API for AMDTP admission fluctuates, depending on the number of available slots in the program, and the number of assholes needed, at the time.

Once the candidate has been approved for admission into the AMDTP, they need to be slotted into the correct module, based on their personality.

Since all of this is based on how the candidate looks on paper and in interviews, not in real business situations, things get interesting when the wrong person, as happens often at the dysfunctional company, is slotted in the wrong AMDTP module.

Hierarchy of Course Modules in the AMDTP

The following are the six magic modules in the AMDTP course, ranked from the most to the least prestigious:

1. The Megalomanic
2. The Wizard
3. The Sky Watcher
4. The Desk Slammer
5. The Micromanager
6. The Village Idiot

The Megalomaniac

The Megalomaniac is the king of beasts in the AMDTP. He or she is only interested in their own personal power. Their only goal is to rise to the top of the company pyramid and will stop at nothing to get there. Once there, they already have their sights set on their next move. They only see the dysfunctional company as the next step in their path to world domination. Today the dysfunctional company, tomorrow the world.

The Megalomaniac has an inexhaustible ego needing constant feeding. Power is their addiction, and power is more addictive than any narcotic.

The Megalomaniac can never get enough. The ideal candidate for The Megalomaniac slot is self-centered and, ideally, should also be a narcissist and a sociopath. Personality tests should also show candidates to be arrogant and cold-hearted, two other traits required for The Megalomaniac position.

The Megalomaniac sees everybody at the company, both their direct reports and others, not as humans, but as objects to be manipulated and exploited for their own personal gain. Anybody can be stepped on or pushed aside, when necessary. Since the dysfunctional company is only a stepping stone, they don't value the company either, except for how it furthers their naked – or more likely, clothed – ambitions.

Fellow employees and management? Customers? The public? The common good? They're all afterthoughts. The Megalomaniac is only about taking from the company – and everybody else – and not giving back. It's a one-way street for The Megalomaniac.

The Megalomaniac can be easily spotted in the office, or on video calls. They have their nose in the air and are often wearing a cape and a crown. Some will even carry around a scepter with an orb for added effect. They're arrogant and thoughtless with no concern for what others think. They're accountable to nobody but themselves.

Everybody around them must remember to kiss the ring, or else face retribution. They want to be feared, not loved. The Megalomaniac will always remind everybody at the company who they are. They always say, "Don't you know who I am?" – a rhetorical question The Megalomaniac has already asked a thousand times.

If anybody questions their authority, they drop a name or two of someone higher up to impress and intimidate. The Megalomaniac is always well-connected or, at least, appears to be so. Anybody who crosses swords with The Megalomaniac, does so at their own risk. Many have been beheaded for less.

Their video calls always have power backgrounds with a picture of themselves atop a mountain, complete with hiking gear, ski googles and trekking poles, or crossing a finish line at an athletic event. They must always be the center of attention. "Did you really climb Mount Everest?" "Is that really you at the Olympics?" It's far more important to be seen at meetings than to actually conduct the meeting or, has been seen in Habit Four, get anything accomplished.

The Megalomaniac, also called **The Little Dictator**, or **The Little General**, can be seen ordering people around, their favorite activity. The Megalomaniac would rather boss people around all day than get any productive work done. They love power games and shows of force. They love building their little internal empires.

After all, every self-respecting Megalomanic knows the rule at the dysfunctional company from Habit Two: headcount = power.

The AMDTP training teaches The Megalomaniac how to balance their insatiable appetite for power with the need to sometimes be The Body Cutter. The Megalomaniac needs to learn when to grow their team, and when to let go. Laying off employees should be second nature to The Megalomaniac.

The Megalomaniac may be called upon to commit merciless bloodletting. Mass layoffs are part of their job description. The Megalomaniac warms up between mass layoffs by firing people individually on the spot in front of the team for something minor – like sneezing or yawning. Summary dismissals is just another power game for The Megalomaniac. They love publicly humiliating their own staff, or anybody else, for that matter.

Blackmail: A Management Tool to Control Employees

Blackmail is another effective tool The Megalomaniac uses to control difficult members of their team. For example, every Megalomaniac has a hidden list, updated monthly, of who is sleeping with whom. It's strongly recommended not to share this with HR. It should be The Megalomaniac's little secret, brought out at appropriate times for disciplining recalcitrant employees.

Of course, in more straightlaced companies this information might be harder to dig up but, not surprisingly, might actually be more frequent. The stuffed shirts and bras just hide it better. In any case, if the company is dysfunctional, promiscuity is sure to follow. It's a way employees blow off steam from long hours in meetings, low productivity and low morale so common at the dysfunctional company.

On the other hand, sexual activity on the premises should be strongly discouraged, just like the prohibition on yoga and meditation in FFZs. These activities only releases tension, which could lead to an unhealthy rise in productivity. And this, of course, is strictly unacceptable in the dysfunctional company.

Mass layoffs and blackmail are all in a day's work for the dysfunctional company's super hero.

The Megalomaniac is often nicknamed God's Gift. They think their exceptional management skill makes them God's Gift to the company. They think they're so talented, nobody can touch them, literally. They think they know everything about not only the company but also the business. This overlaps with The Wizard and The Know-It-All, as will be seen shortly, saving the company training costs of putting The Megalomaniac candidate through cross-training in other AMDTP modules.

The Wizard

The Wizard is short for The Wizard of Bullshit. The Wizard is also known as The Know-It-All. The Wizard never asks questions, because, well, The Wizard already knows all the answers. They know everything and will impress everybody at the dysfunctional company with their encyclopedic knowledge about some subject or, maybe even every subject. Just ask them. They would be happy to talk to – or rather, talk at – anybody.

The ideal candidate for The Wizard of Bullshit is an attention-starved manager with a fragile ego who needs to show off. Those with higher degrees, including frustrated MBAs who think they're underemployed, also make good candidates. They feel their education gave them the skills – even though they don't have the experience – entitling them to be in upper management.

When The Wizard doesn't have an answer, which is rare, they fling bullshit around until it sticks. They're master con artists who fool everybody into thinking they're the world's authority – on everything. They not only bore their team with details – sometimes too explicit – about their travels, they also claim to know how to fly the plane. The Wizard, of course, is the Center of All Known Knowledge in the Universe.

With their vast store of knowledge, The Wizard can be mistaken for God's Gift. The Wizard has some God's Gift tendencies, for sure. But The Wizard is still lower in the food chain than The Megalomaniac, where God's Gift usually resides. While The Wizard has valuable knowledge and skills or, at least, fakes it well, he or she lacks the inflated ego needed for The Megalomaniac track.

Another name for the The Wizard is The Pompous Windbag. The Wizard Windbag pontificates on and on and on and on – seemingly endlessly – about bullshit long after everybody has stopped listening. Meanwhile, he or she demands complete attention. Anybody caught falling asleep, or even staring at the wall or ceiling, will be sent to HR for punishment for insubordination or worse, off to a company correction camp (see Habit Three) for indoctrination on blind obedience to management.

A favorite sport of The Pompous Windbag side of The Wizard is the game of "Can You Top This?" Whatever anybody says they've accomplished something, The Windbag will always respond with something bigger or better.

Two Executives Walk into a Bar . . .

Two executives go into a bar. One says, "I laid off an entire department and saved the company tons of money." The Windbag executive answers, "Yeah, but I've laid off more people in my entire career here than you ever will. Nah, nah, nah, nah, nah. I laid off accounting before you even thought of it. Who needs those depressing bean counters always telling us we're losing money?"

By the time they're stone drunk, they've laid off the entire company, in the popular game at the dysfunctional company: Who Can Lay Off More Employees? Body counts from layoffs are big bragging rights for The Cabal at the dysfunctional company.

The Wizard is always in self-promotion mode and is, of course, always perfect. He or she never met a mirror they didn't like. They can be identified in the office by their constant preening in the hall or at their PAWS. If no mirror is nearby, they always have one handy in their pocket.

Some are also known as Chest Slammers, from beating their chests, while saying how great they are. As that famous chest beater, Tarzan, used to say, the dysfunctional equivalent, The Wizard says – "Me Wizard. You lowly employee."

The Sky Watcher

The next layer down in the AMDTP food chain is **The Sky Watcher**. The Sky Watcher has elements of both The Megalomaniac and The Wizard but is lower down in the dysfunctional hierarchy and is often a vice president, director or even a manager looking for a boost up the next rung – or two or three – of the ladder.

The Sky Watcher is someone in management and above, who only manages up, never down. In a functional company, a good manager is skilled at managing both up and down the hierarchy. They know how to be both the manager and the managed. They know how to simultaneously oversee their team effectively, while navigating the waters above their head to get things done. They dance the delicate dance between those they manage and being managed themselves.

They respect both those who report to them and those to whom they report. Not in the dysfunctional company, where The Sky Watcher only respects those above, while disrespecting those below.

The Sky Watcher only does half the job of managing. They treat their underlings like dirt, if they pay attention to them, at all. They're too busy ass-kissing their supervisors. The Sky Watcher is infamous for taking credit for everything, while never acknowledging the hard work, or any work, at all, for that matter, of anyone on their team.

The Sky Watcher is sometimes called The Slacker Climber, who is only interested in high profile projects but does no work and then mysteriously gets ahead. They look good but there is nothing behind the veneer. Not surprisingly, The Slacker Climber is the most often to be promoted in the dysfunctional company.

The Sky Watcher can be seen in the office with their lips surgically attached to the rear end of their supervisor. If The Sky Watcher is remote, they will always have their boss's chat window open, so they can chime in anytime with this or that great achievement. The Sky Watcher is the consummate sycophant and yes-man. The Sky Watcher is the boss's pet.

The Sky Watcher is often as equally ruthless as The Megalomaniac but lower in rank. Just like The Megalomaniac, they see each new position as only a stepping stone to the next position. Also like The Megalomaniac, The Sky Watcher is armed with their dagger hidden in their briefcase, or buried in a spreadsheet, ready to back stab at any moment.

The Desk Slammer

The Desk Slammer is just a hot head. They're always hitting their desks, or shaking their fist in the air, angry at something or somebody. They're never happy. Whatever their team is doing, it's not enough. In fact, it's never enough.

The Desk Slammer is **The Screamer and Yeller**, walking around the office, or in their online chat, always yelling. "More, more, more," is a favorite. They can be polite: "You call this crap that you did 'work'?" Or they can be direct, even profane: "Do you know what the f*** you're doing?" However, they express themselves, it's always loud and belligerent. Screaming is their normal tone of voice.

Screamers and Yellers have only two emotions: quiet and angry. Anger helps carry them through the rare moments of quiet. They're perfectionists.

They're always critical. Nothing is ever good enough. If nothing is ever good enough, then nothing gets done. This leads to a lot of hard work with no results – The Principle of the Appearance of Activity in action.

The normal day at the dysfunctional company is already full of aggravation and drama. The Desk Slammer takes advantage of every stage call to perform and then creates more drama to makes things worse. The Desk Slammer doesn't need an opportunity to pop their cork. They do it naturally, all the time.

The Desk Slammer always thinks the sky is falling. They go non-stop from crisis to crisis. The Desk Slammer is never calm. The Desk Slammer is also **The Doomsday Prophet**, or **The Naysayer**. They're always negative. Everything is bad. They spread gloom and doom throughout the office and, of course, The Naysayer's answer to every question is "no." They love to spread rumors about how this or that idea will never work and will only destroy the team, if not the company.

The Desk Slammer never approves anything without some drama, usually screaming and yelling. Budgets? The Desk Slammer is also **The Skin Flint** and **The Tight Wad**. They think they're the vanguard of the fiscal castle, which the Cabal is too busy raiding to even notice The Desk Slammer's penny pinching.

What about money for something helpful, like membership in an industry trade association or maybe for attending a conference where they could learn about their competition? Let employees stay in the dark. Let them be ignorant about the industry. How about a little petty cash for pizzas during meetings? Forget it. Let the staff go hungry.

The Screamer and Yeller is a frustrated low-level employee who feels oppressed by the many layers of management above them.

Before all offices – even dysfunctional ones – went smoke free, The Desk Slammer could be seen chomping on a cigar and spitting out tobacco. Today, **The Cigar Chomper** can vent all their hostility personally, or in online chats, at employees. They don't need special smoking sanctuaries to abuse employees. They can now do it out in the open, in fresh air.

The Desk Slammer isn't a nice person – period. For that matter, then, nobody else in the AMDTP is either. It would make sense to have a management program for mentally stable and down-to-earth employees interested in building the business. Not the dysfunctional company. The

AMDTP was designed with the power-hungry psycho and deranged sociopath in mind.

The last two slots in the AMDTP – The Micromanager and The Village Idiot – exist at all levels and are always part of another AMDTP modules. The Megalomaniac, for example, might also be The Micromanager or, possibly, even The Village Idiot. Likewise, The Sky Watcher could also be The Village Idiot. The possibilities to mix and match these types is exhausting, just like their behavior.

Whatever their slot in the program, they're still equally vital in the AMDTP approach to building dysfunctional management.

The Micromanager

The Micromanager is like mold. They grow everywhere. They're peering over employees' shoulders at their PAWS, watching them online through their laptop or from surveillance cameras overhead, listening in from garbage cans or, if they're real perverts, looking up skirts from below. Just like mold, they're a nuisance that spreads and never goes away.

They're in everybody's business all the time. They fire questions too rapidly for their team to answer.

Instead of helping, they're a roadblock, keeping anybody from getting anything done with their incessant meddling. They stir up activity but get no results, per The Principle of the Appearance of Activity.

The Micromanager must always know every detail at every moment of everything going on. They demand reports every nanosecond about every activity, including bio and snack breaks. Nothing is too small to not be recorded. If someone steps out to the bathroom, it must be noted – in detail.

The Micromanager must be copied on every e-mail, be on every call and attend every meeting, even if only virtually or by teleconference. Afterward, they must always add their "thoughts." They're like a quiet Desk Slammer. They're perfectionists. Everything must be done their way – or no way. Deep down, they just want to push their team away and do the work themselves. The Micromanager then wonders why they're overworked.

The Micromanager, like The Wizard, is always right. Everybody else is always wrong. Nobody, except for The Micromanager themself, of course, knows how to do anything correctly.

The Micromanager thinks they can both conduct the orchestra and play an instrument. They don't understand you can't do both. You either have to manage or do the work. The concept of leadership without interference is foreign to them. The word "delegate" isn't in their vocabulary.

The motto of The Micromanager is, "If I want something done, I have to do it myself."

The Village Idiot

The Village Idiot, as the name implies, is, well, just a moron. These creatures can be found throughout the dysfunctional company. Candidates for this program must be below a certain IQ. They have an IQ ceiling, above which they can't exceed, rather than an IQ floor, which for normal jobs, and normal employees, would be the minimum grey matter required for the position.

The Village Idiot is basically out of touch with reality – a trait common to all AMDTP enrollees – besides being just plain stupid. They have no idea what they're doing. They don't understand the company and its business, and they usually don't understand their industry either.

Unfortunately, they got into the AMDTP because they won the right turf battles, have the right political connections, or because of simple nepotism. Office politics guarantees their place is secure in the dysfunctional company. They can't be dislodged until it's too late, often only when the ship is already sinking.

The Village Idiot can be spotted always asking for help. Some may be slick enough to ask without showing their ignorance. Some may be polite. Others may be downright nasty, default dysfunctional company behavior. Still others may just be The Megalomaniac in disguise, playing dumb to steal valuable information.

Only The Megalomaniac would pose as The False Village Idiot. The Wizard's and The Sky Watcher's big egos and pride prevent them from condescending to ask for anything. The Desk Slammer and The Micromanager are just too busy hammering their team.

The Village Idiot, sometimes also called **The Clueless Moron**, is at every level in the dysfunctional company. They could be a figurehead CEO brought in from outside for window dressing and ribbon-cutting down to a politically-appointed manager with no experience.

Whatever their slot, AMDTP graduates have been finally initiated into the great fraternity who all learn the same thing, as indicated by the motto in small print on the bottom of their completion certificate:

Only Assholes Get Ahead Here

How AMDTP Removes Competent Executives

There are executives in normal companies who genuinely earned their stripes by working their way up the organization. They started at the bottom in the lowest imaginable jobs. They may have swept the floor, been a cashier or took orders. They may have worked in the mail room, on the loading dock, drove a truck or been an assistant or gopher. They may have been low-level IT staff who improved their skills and built up their technical toolbox on the job, learning something new every step along the way.

They moved up because they demonstrated leadership and competence even in the lowliest, least paid activities. On their way up, they moved around, learning marketing here, finance there, and operations somewhere in between.

They didn't puff themselves up to get promoted. They didn't play politics. They quietly observed the company and its competition. They learned strategy through doing business. They learned business by doing business, not through building fiefs and walls and moats.

Ultimately, by the time they got to the top, they learned everything they could about the company, its business and how it operates. They truly love the company and want it to succeed and serve its customers.

There are other executives in normal companies who may have come in sideways, at a mid-level or higher, from outside. They may not have worked their way up, but they may have had certain expertise the company lacked. It could be something technical. It could be specialized knowledge of the product or service. They may be recognized geniuses in their field. They may have advanced degrees relevant to the company. Unlike The Wizard, however, they don't flash their degrees around.

These enlightened executives may also have people skills to match to get everybody in the company on board during implementation of tough, but necessary, measures. They make intelligent decisions and then carefully explain to fellow executives, managers and employees how their decision, even if unpopular, will benefit them and the company as a whole.

The dysfunctional company, on the other hand, isn't a normal company.

The dysfunctional company doesn't want these types of executives. They must be removed for the good of the feudal lords running the show. They get in the way of the empire builders and the pocket liners. As was seen in Habit Six, the dysfunctional company drives out its best employees. AMDTP takes it to the next level as the vehicle for expelling its best executives. Its sole purpose is to complete the purge of excellence from the company.

There are cab drivers and hair dressers and small shop owners with more business sense than some dysfunctional company executives. They know how to sell and market – on their own. They know how to hire and fire the right staff – on their own. They know how to manage finances – on their own. They don't have armies of useless consultants and know-nothing staff to back them up.

The dysfunctional executive? They couldn't even run a corner lemonade stand. Selling lemonade just gets in the way of meetings and sending out silly pronouncements by e-mail, or drafting idiotic policies irrelevant to the business.

They wouldn't have anybody in the lemonade stand to push around. They wouldn't have anybody to do their dirty work. They might actually, for once, have to do some real work. They might have to wear an apron and actually talk to customers. They might have to think about marketing instead of turf building.

They might have to think about the business instead of how they look in the mirror.

The Final Act: The Bureapocalypse

The dysfunctional company is now complete. Its best executives driven out by AMDTP, its best employees driven out by HR, it's now ready for its final act in disservice to the community. It's alumni are now ready to be unleashed into the world.

They all learned the dysfunctional company's most important lessons, suitable for framing as a plaque in their PAWS:

> *Talented, creative, innovative, or*
> *enthusiastic people can't get ahead.*
> *Ego and power are everything.*
> *You have to be an asshole to succeed.*

Along the way, they watched helplessly as the bureaucrats replaced the businesspeople.

They saw businesspeople create products and services and reach out to customers.
They then saw bureaucrats create paperwork and hierarchies and look inward.

They saw businesspeople lower roadblocks and build bridges.
They then saw bureaucrats raise barricades and build walls.

They saw businesspeople produce business and customers and revenue.
They then saw bureaucrats waste time and energy with useless rules.

They then saw the **Bureapocalypse** approaching.

The sky is getting dark and vultures are circling overhead. The competition is stealing customers. Sales are falling. The balance sheet is shrinking. The earth is trembling. The dysfunctional company's foundation is cracking. The pyramid built to last an eternity is shaky.

The rain is pounding harder. Thunder and lightning have started. The black clouds are thickening. The sky is getting darker.

The **Bureapocalypse** is getting closer.

Yet the brain surgeons in the executive suite still can't see or don't understand, or don't want to understand, or don't want to face reality. They believe their own poor communication. They believe their own propaganda. They believe their own lies. Everything still looks great from their fortress insulated from employees, customers, and the rest of the world.

Some employees on the front lines and in the bureaucratic trenches are astute enough to see what is happening. Some are aware enough to get out in time. Others are either blindsided or, like their executive superiors, in a self-delusional fog.

The rest have lost hope and just don't care anymore. They started polishing their resumes long ago, getting prepared for the inevitable and their next move.

The **Bureapocalypse** is closing in.

The bureaucracy has hardened up. It can't move. The dysfunctional company can't innovate. It can't get anything done, even to save itself from disaster.

Then, finally, the sky opens up and a massive thunderbolt comes down. The ground below opens up and the whole edifice collapses and falls into a giant sinkhole, disappearing into the earth, never to be seen again.

The **Bureapocalypse** has arrived.

The executives who jettisoned with golden parachutes are gone. It doesn't matter now anyways. It's too late. No leadership. No management. They had abandoned both long ago.

The rest of the AMDTP graduates, the vice presidents, directors, managers and their hangers-on and the remaining employees, and whoever can scramble for lifeboats, will all live another day only to be reunited again at the next dysfunctional gig.

Future archaeologists will unearth the ruins of the dysfunctional company and will wonder how people survived in little rabbit hutches known as their PAWS.

Appendices:

Acronym Dictionary
Dysfunctional Psalm

"You mean we have to put up with more crap . . ."

Acronym Dictionary

ACF
Asshole Customer Factor
The percentage of asshole customers contacting
Customer Disservice per day
Habit Five

ADR
Asshole Density Ratio
A rough indicator of dysfunctionality based on the
percentage of assholes in the company
Introduction

AMDTP
Asshole Management Development Training
Program
The dysfunctional company's training program for
producing ineffective and abusive executives and
managers
Habit Seven

AMP
Acute Meeting Psychosis
Sudden dizzy spells and nausea appearing
unexpectedly during a meeting
Habit Four

API
Asshole Potential Index
Indicator of the level of asshole behavior of a
candidate for the AMDTP
Habit Six

ARA
Asshole Reserve Army
A database of resumes indicating asshole potential
or containing the word "asshole"
Habit Six

ATD
Areas of Total Darkness
Empty and unused office space left abandoned
after a mass layoff
Habit Six

BAR
Bathroom Attendance Ratio
The percentage of time an employee spends in the
bathroom, also used in the annual performance
review
Habit Three

BBT
Business Blocker Twins
The two most common and effective barriers to
productive work: e-mail and meetings
Habit Three

CAR
Customer Acceptance Ratio
The percentage of live calls to Customer Disservice actually reaching an agent
Habit Five

CO
Company Orphan
An employee with no known living, or dead, supervisor or manager who is adrift in the bureaucracy
Habit Six

CUP
Company Underwear Policy
The policy requiring all employees to wear underwear with the company logo at all meetings
Habit Four

DBPP
Death by PowerPoint
The policy requiring the use of PowerPoint instead of white boards at all meetings
Habit Four

DCAC
Dysfunctional Company Acronym Creation
The procedure for developing acronyms as part of, or to replace, Company Speak
Habit Three

DNRP

Duplicate Name Reduction Program

The removal of employees with duplicate surnames to reduce e-mail clutter and redundancy

Habit Three

D&R

Dump and Run

Sending out a sensitive or annoying e-mail at the end of the day and then leaving and ignoring it

Habit Three

EEMF

Executive Equivalency Management Factor

The number of employees whose combined salaries would equal the pay of an executive

Habit Six

ESF

Executive Supplement Factor

The number of executive assholes added to the number of employee assholes to correctly calculate the ADR

Introduction

FFZ

Free Fire Zone

A dedicated area in the office for employees to scream, moan or bang their head to vent their frustrations

Habit Six

FPTTA
False Promotion Through Title Advancement
A promotion in title only with more work but less support and no new staff
Habit Three

HCD
Horizontal Communication Disturbance
Annoying and excessive e-mails between people at the same level of the bureaucracy or hierarchy
Habit Three

HPT
High Priests of Technology
What the Lords of IT call themselves to justify their arrogance toward the company NTMs
Habit Two

HTI
Horizontal Title Inflation
The addition of words to a title in a false promotion to give the false impression of advancement in rank
Habit Three

IRBM
Inter Row Ballistic Missile
A crude weapon made of office supplies for employees to defend their PAWS against intruders
Habit Six

MAR
Meeting Attendance Ratio
The percent of time the employee is in meetings, also part of the annual performance review
Habit Four

MIB
Missing in Bureaucracy
An employee, usually a CO, unable to find themselves on the org chart
Habit Six

MP
Meeting Police
The goons in the hall patrolling the office enforcing mandatory meeting attendance
Habit Four

NTM
Non-Technical Moron
The term used by the Lords of IT to refer to their non-technical co-workers
Habit Two

OBB
Occasional Business Blockers
Dysfunctional business units sometimes preventing productive work, often audit and legal departments
Habit One

PAWS
Pre-Assigned Workstation
The fundamental building block of the dysfunctional company usually consisting of open workspaces or cubicles where employees work
Introduction

PIC
Pre-Irritated Customer
A customer already hot and bothered before even contacting Customer Disservice
Habit Five

RC
Row Captain
Leader of each row of PAWSs responsible for maintaining row discipline, storing used pizza boxes and handling deceased employees at their desks
Habit Six

REC
Reverse Elbow Curl
A non-violent way for an employee to defuse an aggravating incident without leaving their PAWS
Habit Six

REUC
Remote Employee Dress Code
The policy requiring all remote employees to be clothed during video conference calls
Habit Four

SLOC
Standing Lavatory Observation Committee
A TWM for reviewing bathrooms and making sure they are clean and functional
Habit One

TWM
The Weekly Meeting
A Weekly meeting serving no purpose other than to tie up employees, inflict pain and cause mental illness
Habit One

UBA
Unproductive Bureaucratic Activity
Amount of time spent on nonsensical bureaucratic support activities, also used in the annual performance review
Habit Six

USA
Unproductive Socializing Activity
Amount of time spent on forced socializing activities and chatting, also used in the annual performance review
Habit Six

VCD
<u>Vertical Communication Disturbance</u>
Annoying and excessive e-mails between people at
different levels of the bureaucracy or hierarchy
Habit Three

VTI
<u>Vertical Title Inflation</u>
A promotion with minimal changes to the title
Habit Three

The Dysfunctional Psalm

The Company is my shepherd; I shall not want.

It maketh me to sit in rows of work spaces: it leadeth me into meeting rooms.

It restoreth my migraine: it leadeth me to bang my head against the wall for the Company's sake.

Yea, though I walk through the valley of auditors, I will fear no finding: for my manager will be taken down with me; thy e-mail chain and thy paper trail they comfort me.

Thou preparest a way before me in the presence of mine bureaucracy; thou anointest my head with an inhumane workload; my video calls runneth over.

Surely e-mail and meetings shall follow me all the days of my work: and I will dwell in my cubicle of the Company until I am laid off.

Source: Adapted from Psalm 23 of the King James Version

Made in the USA
Columbia, SC
04 July 2024

9a6ec870-438f-46ce-b8f3-abf9f6f47ce7R03

3